Person-Centred Approaches in Schools

Jackie Hill

PCCS BOOKS

Manchester

First published in 1994
PCCS BOOKS
Paragon House
Seymour Grove
Old Trafford
Manchester
M16 0LN

Person-Centred Approaches in Schools

ISBN 1 898059 07 1

Printed by Printoff Graphic Arts Ltd., Alexander House,
Lomeshaye Road, Nelson, Lancashire.

Contents

If........

If you are a happy teacher, working in a happy school, with happy children.....

If you feel that you are not constrained by outside forces over which you have no control.....

If you feel satisfied by the job you do.....

If there is a place for your professional, and personal, development.....

If you have a person to whom you can turn if you have a need.....

If the children you work with are all achieving their maximum potential and are developing as well-rounded individuals.....

If there is no 'sickness' or stress in your school.....

If the children all arrive with breakfast inside them, with money or food for lunch, in clean clothes, without any bruises, and with a light heart.....

If the people in your school never feel ill, sad, ecstatic, depressed, or worried.....

If you never feel that it's the kids and not you in control.....

If there is room for the views, the personalities, the quirks of all.....

If there is no prejudice about sex, race, class, style of ear-rings, types of trainers, leather elbow patches, weight, glasses, buck teeth, spots, stammerers.....

.....then this book is not for you.

"Certainly education as I had experienced it had done very little to teach me how to know what I really wanted, but a great deal to lead me into accepting what other people wanted, while making believe that it was my own wish: in fact, it had been a very effective education in self-deception."
Joanna Field (Marion Milner) *'An Experiment in Leisure,'* Virago 1986.

Extract reproduced by kind permission of the publishers Virago Press.

Introduction

About this book

I had three aims in writing this book. The first was to draw attention to the full extent of a teacher's job and the fact that most of us are only trained to carry out half of it; the half of it that relates to the tangibles of academic learning or acquiring specific skills like playing an instrument, holding a racquet or making biscuits.

But there are the intangibles that children learn too. These are not necessarily taught consciously or actively but are learnt almost accidentally. This hidden curriculum includes survival in groups of varying sizes, learning how to respond appropriately in a large institution, how to placate the school bully, or con their way to the front of the dinner queue. More importantly they add to their learning about who they are and where they fit in. This learning is of vital importance in a child's wider education; some might even say that it is of more importance than that which is on the timetable. And if the learning on this hidden curriculum is to happen beneficially and not in a way that leaves scars, I believe that it needs to be as closely managed, planned for and monitored as the National Curriculum.

There can be little doubt that schools play a major part in the way children learn to understand themselves and relate to others, and teachers need to be trained to identify and facilitate this process. If teachers are expected to be responsible for developing qualities such as creativity and sensitivity, confidence and moral behaviour, we need to be well trained and able to practise what we preach.

School education is experiencing a time of great change. The National Curriculum, attainment targets, records of achievement and league tables have all focused attention on not only the academic successes of the pupils but also on their behaviour. The general drift of public opinion seems to be finding standards of achievement and behaviour below what they expect. Standards are perceived to be slipping and there are serious attempts to reverse the apparent down-ward slide But I think it is counter-productive for anyone to try to put the clock back to the time when children seemed to do as they were told. That is simply avoiding responsibility. Helping children to grow into mature adults requires a far more subtle approach than a return to Victorian values. If Victorian values worked at all it was through fear and control. Do we want to frighten our children into submission or coerce them to act in an acceptable manner? If we don't, then we need another strategy.

My second aim is to demonstrate that the person-centred approach to education is feasible, practical and helpful. It can clarify and deal with many of the grey areas that fall outside the curriculum but which have a crucial impact on a child's (and everybody else's) experience of school. It provides a structure, a way of understanding, and methods for dealing with, areas such as relationships, emotional development and ethical behaviour that seem to be at the root of most of the problems experienced in school and society at large.

And thirdly, I want to show that getting Back to Basics *is* the answer. I believe that getting Back to Basics will improve a school's performance; the truancy rates will drop and exam results will improve. But the basics I think we should get back to are the principles that tell us that each person is of equal value. For me, it means treating people with respect, not judging them but giving them space to be their own, unique selves. In other words, getting back to basics means being **Person-Centred**.

This book is about person-centredness and to be true to those principles I have tried to write it in a person-centred way. I do not put myself forward as an expert, and where I offer ways to tackle things, they are not just my own, but also come from the many committed people who have practised a person-centred way of being over the years. It is my intention to share with you what I have found useful in the hope that you will find something within these pages that 'speaks to your condition' and that you can be of use to you. During my years of study I have read much research and while it has been interesting and informative I tend to rely on the wisdom of my senses and experiences, as we can all do. I want to encourage teachers to trust their own understanding of their world and to do what they think is best for themselves and the people they teach and work with; to put gut-feeling back in there amongst the vast amount of research, theory, Politics and politics.

Current examples of the person-centred approach

The person-centred approach has filtered through to the educational world to some extent already. As early as 1963, the Newson report recommended the employment of school counsellors. If you look around the country these ideas are proving their worth in many different ways and contexts. The education services in Dudley in the West Midlands include a counselling service to help children with emotional or behaviour problems function effectively in school. Staff in the counselling service are trained both as teachers and counsellors and they aim to provide a service that offers counselling to pupils and staff, Inset training for teachers and a facility for school refusers. Some schools have their staff trained in counselling skills whilst others consider themselves child-centred.

In the North West of England, Manchester based its teacher appraisal programme on the person-centred model. There are universities and colleges that use a student-lead learning approach. In talking to some of the people involved I have found that they feel as though they have a valuable tool to help them do their job more effectively.

The Alfred Barrow School in Barrow-in-Furness has a person-centred approach to bullying. The policy arose out of a school-wide concern and was developed in co-operation with everyone in the school. They regard themselves as a 'telling school' where the children are encouraged to tell someone if they are being bullied. Once they have 'told' then they are instantly believed and their wishes for action are acted upon where possible. If the bullied child considers it appropriate a meeting is set up with the bully and both parties are encouraged to express their feelings while the others listen and without blame being laid at anyone's door. Solutions are discussed and agreed to by all concerned; the aim being a win-win situation where everybody's needs are considered and where possible attended to.

Since the 80s the impetus to make education more child-centred has tailed off leaving us with a piecemeal, 'make it up as you go along' approach to relationships in schools. Sometimes the term child-centred is used without the implications for the education of the whole child being fully understood, and there is often confusion between the role of a counsellor and teachers who have counselling skills. But there are those who believe, even more strongly in the climate of the 90s, that a model for counselling can, and should, become the basis of an educational approach.

Who is the book for?

This book is for those who....
....have disruptive children in their classes,
....see children who are bullied,
....feel bullied themselves,
....find certain staff difficult to work with,
....have difficulties getting support from parents,

....find difficulty in motivating certain pupils,
....witness conflicts,
....get drawn into conflicts,
....feel lacking in confidence,
....find being in school a brutalising experience at times,
....just want to improve the quality of their relationships.

If you are an ordinary teacher working in an ordinary school......

.......then this book is for you!

The issues in this book are for all people who work in a school no matter how great or small their experience. Situations in schools are constantly changing and every time we meet new pupils, or staff, we have to start from scratch to build a relationship with them before effective teaching can begin. And, of course, it will become obvious to you as you read the book that what lies in these pages is of universal use to us in the whole of our daily lives, in fact any time we make contact with another person that contact will be enhanced by bearing person-centred values in mind.

What can the book do for you?

Whether you feel overwhelmed by problems in your teaching life, powerless to change anything, or just want to make some changes in the way you relate to your pupils, this book has something to offer you. If you start, you will meet up with others of a like mind and begin to develop a support network for yourself. It is better to have at least tried to do something to change the present state of affairs, where many people feel adrift in a world that seems to be full of inconsistencies, injustice and cruelty. I would even go so far as to say that all people-problems in school will be helped by using a person-centred approach to them. The skills outlined in this book.can be used to deal with truancy, bullying, poor motivation, poor performance and conflict.

If you feel your control is diminishing, or you feel deskilled by expectations to perform, or overburdened by social problems children bring to you and your lessons then this book will provide you with a means to tackle those issues and return to you some feeling that *you can do something about it.*

I feel it is important to state here that this book is not designed to turn teachers into psychotherapists or social workers. There are already people trained to do those jobs. A teacher's job is to 'educate' the children they have in their charge. Pupils aren't just empty vessels to be filled however; teaching cannot take place without the willingness to learn and learning takes place best within sound relationships. This book is to help teachers do their job more effectively.

How to use the book

The following chapters contain many common sense, practical suggestions for ways you can implement a change in relationships in your classroom and your school. To help you make these changes there are suggestions for training, and things for you to think about, scattered throughout the text for you to use as part of a training programme with groups of other teachers and for you to tussle with by yourself. If however this training opportunity is not immediately open to you you could try to set one up, formally or informally; learning of this sort is best done with others to enable you to practise your relationship skills.

Practically speaking, the ideas in this book can be used in many ways. Individual teachers who develop their communication skills can improve the quality of their relationships, and it can be used to empower all the people in a school, not just the teachers. Children too, will benefit from learning relationship skills as well as from being on the receiving end of them.

Secondary school teachers may be wondering if the ideas in this book can be useful for them. It may be easy to see how PSE teachers can use this type of approach but how will it fit in for busy subject teachers? It will take time to teach children to use and respond to these skills and if it is impossible for it to be timetabled into an already overburdened school-day, Pastoral time with form teachers is an obvious place to build up their skills. But once pupils and staff are used to this way of working it can be called upon at any time, in any lesson, in any situation where a problem appears.

You may of course be one of only a few teachers in your school - don't despair if this is the case. You can still be person-centred in your own dealings with the people you meet during your day; it may be a little more difficult to get any support that you need but teachers are famously resourceful and no doubt you will find a way to work that suits you and your situation.

****

Remember it takes time and courage to change the way you relate to others and you need to be able to be kind to yourself and tolerant of mistakes that you will surely make along the way. Don't be disheartened if things take a long time or if things don't turn out the way you planned; changes such as these can cause much resistance from unwilling colleagues and pupils but perseverance will pay in the end. Congratulate yourself for your achievements, however small; and give yourself the first pat on the back for picking up this book!

The Whole Job 1

Teaching : only the half of it.

When I left teacher training college, I had passed exams in the history and philosophy of education, learnt how to plan my lessons, and understood the importance of using interesting and relevant teaching materials. And apart from experiencing a few twinges of uncertainty during teaching practice, I felt enthusiastic and well-prepared for my first job.

But of course it wasn't that easy. The reality of working with my first class of children was daunting. The fact that they might have had a different agenda from mine had not entered my head. And even if it had, my training had given me the impression that any failure to learn could be remedied by good teaching.

What about all those issues that had to be addressed before I could even start to teach? How did I actually gain the respect of my pupils? How did I get them to listen to me and to do the things I asked them to do without having to shout, threaten or nag? Reality too, put me in touch with all sorts of grey areas in my thinking that I had not been aware of before. I was confused about my role; how familiar should I let the children be? How much choice should I allow them? Would encouraging their independence threaten my authority?

Teaching was only the half of it. I had somehow to make a relationship with the children in my class. In spite of three years training, the only role-models I had of this were my own school teachers.

In Training
Share with the others in a group how well prepared you felt when you first started teaching? What were your biggest concerns? What were the biggest surprises?

Teachers do much more than simply educate children during 1265 hours and 190 days of directed time. As it states in our job description, we are responsible for 'promoting the progress and well-being' of our pupils. Yet some of the skills required to live up to such a job description have not been given the emphasis they merit in teacher training programmes, nor are they developed as an on-going process during our careers.

In school, children have their first experience of the world outside their family circle. As children grow older, school sets a tone for the way they perceive themselves in relation to society. If we want to promote the well-being of our pupils, we need to be able to 'manage' children in a way that encourages their self-respect and a respect for others and authority. If a child feels valued at school, they will have more chance of perceiving themselves as a valued member of society. This kind of learning takes place on many levels; levels which often get lost under the requirements of the National Curriculum and Attainment Targets.

Teachers need to develop the self-esteem and self-discipline of pupils who have differing abilities and personalities. They also need to create a climate which fosters their pupils' curiosity and ability to think and discuss. People may be aware of the physical and intellectual demands of teaching, but the interpersonal skills required are rarely acknowledged even within the profession itself.

It's becoming increasingly difficult for teachers to feel proud of the profession. The satisfaction of a classroom humming with busy and engaged children, that makes teaching worthwhile, has been eroded by the overwhelming amount of administration and the struggle of getting the children in the right frame of mind to want to learn. The excitement of computer games, TV and videos is making me rethink what I have to offer by comparison. I feel I am groping in the dark, like everyone else, with issues such as bullying, truancy and vandalism, but feeling guilty because I am expected to know the answers and to solve the problems.

It is very tempting for people to look back to the past when children 'did as they were told' and blame today's problems on the absence of corporal punishment. But although fear may succeed in controlling others, for myself, I want a way of relating to young people without having to control them with threats that frighten or shame them. I want to work in a climate of trust. At the same time, I do not want the children to be in control or for me to be colluding with unacceptable behaviour. I want an approach that enables me to relate to young people in such a way that we all keep our self-respect.

The other half of it

Several years ago, I became interested in group work and counselling whilst working alongside social workers in the youth justice centre where I work. Even though I was employed as a teacher, there were times when young people needed counselling and I was also required to join in the group work sessions. So I decided to train as a counsellor.

It was whilst training as a counsellor that I realised that the skills I was learning were what I needed when I left college. They were as useful in my day to day teaching as in my group work and counselling sessions. I realised that I could use other communication skills too, such as assertiveness and negotiation techniques. These skills are frequently used in industry as a basis for training employees who work with the public, in personnel and management, so why not for teachers; we have to 'manage' people too! Education is a two-way process and teachers need to be good role-models for the young people they work with. Communication skills are an important way of empowering teachers and pupils and of avoiding and settling conflict.

I would like to feel that training is available which considers the changes in society and the complexities of the job. If we are responsible for the well-being of our pupils, why was that aspect of the work ignored in my training? Now I find myself feeling that whole areas of my work go unsupported, unvalued and unrecognised in any league tables.

If we want to change things we are going to have to do it from within, and we have to take advantage of developments in training in communication skills. We are also going to have to admit that some young people dislike school and that we have something to do with that state of affairs. There are some people who suggest that schools contribute as much as home background towards failure in children - a sobering thought!

This book is my attempt to draw attention to the fact that it is possible to build on the skills we already have and to change things even if initially only in our own classrooms. There is a range of skills we can use to communicate with others which increase confidence and reduce stress and conflict and so make our teaching more effective. These skills are not only interesting and enjoyable but useful in all areas of life and in personal development. Counselling training gave me insight and understanding of the principles at work in communication and strategies for dealing with the situations at work where relationships and people's problems were involved. By feeling able to create a more relaxed environment in the classroom, I felt better about myself and by understanding the nature of relationships, I was less confused about what I was actually supposed to be doing, because at last I had the tools I needed to do a proper teaching job.

The Person-Centred Approach

2

It is as important for teachers to develop their inter-personal skills as it is for them to know their subject. One of the main reasons people give up on teaching is because they experience difficulties in their relationships with children or their colleagues.

Patterns of communication are not random, they follow certain clearly defined principles. The more we understand about communication, the more we can increase our repertoire of skills. In recent years there has been much interest in counselling and interpersonal skills as a way of improving communication. They form the basis of much of the training used in both industry and the caring professions in areas such as conflict resolution, management, interview techniques and appraisal systems.

Interpersonal skills training is quite different from academic training. It is experiential, learning grows out of self awareness and insight. Communication is a spontaneous, intuitive activity, it isn't possible to memorise techniques for every occasion. Effectivene skilled communication is gained by identification and practice of interpersonal skills, and through exploration of reactions and feelings.

Carl Rogers and the person-centred approach

Carl Rogers, an American psychologist (1902-1987), identified the qualities and skills that were most helpful for counsellors to use with their clients during psychotherapy. He developed a way of working now called person-centred therapy, which proved beneficial for personal development. Rogers realised that person-centredness is a way of *being* that puts people at the centre of any human process and that this way of being could be used for all interpersonal relating.

He deliberately chose to use the words 'counsellor' and 'client' rather than psychotherapist and patient, to model the rightful share of power in the therapeutic relationship: a relationship between equals rather than one having power over the other. However, this has meant that the word counsellor is often mistakenly used as a general term for any professional helpers who use some counselling skills in addition to advice-giving and problem-solving. *It is important to stress that learning counselling skills is not the same as training to become a counsellor, but learning some of the same skills.*

The basis of person-centredness is a respect for individuals, and belief in their value and their potential ability to know what is best for them. If an institution is person-centred it is operated for the benefit of the people it serves and works with them in partnership, along the lines of co-operatives. Such organisations encourage feedback from customers, respect their wishes and do not impose change from above. The same principles apply to person-centred relationships.

To believe that people are capable of making their own decisions requires trust in them and respect for them. It can be difficult to reconcile this belief with our daily experience. Most of the institutions that affect us work on the assumption that experts know better than lay people. This has meant that as institutions have grown bigger the people who make the decisions get further removed from the realities and needs of both their customers and the people who work with them. Procedures tend to be passed down from above, which means that people lower down the hierarchy have less scope for using their professional judgement when they need to respond to the individual needs of the 'customers'. Teachers in particular have less and less space to attend to the specific needs of their pupils. Someone has decided that large schools are the order of the day because they offer more choice to students. However many teachers feel that large schools alienate young people and make it more difficult to develop the social skills which grow out of belonging to a community; interpersonal relationships seem to have suffered in the move towards centralisation of resources.

Person-centredness is a model that can be applied to authorities and institutions so that they become more flexible and 'user-friendly'. More business management is turning its back on the old hierarchical structures and adopting a 'flat' management system where individuals throughout the company are involved in decision-making and responsibility-taking. But it follows that if people begin to trust and believe in themselves, they also have to take responsibility for themselves. It is a big step to let go of the idea that people need to be controlled, or that there are leaders out there, more capable than ordinary people of making the big decisions. Many people are frightened by the idea of making their own decisions, and lack trust that others can do the same. How many people dare challenge the opinion of their doctor, boss or child's teacher unless sorely pressed?

People's dissatisfaction is beginning to bring about change. The obvious effectiveness of self-help groups in such areas as health, housing and personal relationships demonstrates that ordinary people can successfully pool their experiences and come up with pertinent solutions. This change is reflected too, in the 1992 Children's Act which requires that children should be consulted and taken seriously when decisions are being made about their future well-being.

If we want to provide a more beneficial environment in school, we need to understand why these changes are taking place and to dig deeper into human relationships to find out what motivates the behaviour of children, ourselves and others.

Internal motivation

Because we desire the approval of our family, friends and society at large, we are not motivated solely by our impulses towards satisfaction and survival, as animals are. Carl Rogers looked at the way we are influenced by values and perceptions which are passed on to us, without question, from generation to generation. As children, we start to build up our sense of identity and self-worth from the perceptions of ourselves and our behaviour given to us by adults. Adults, however, can't help passing on their standards of what is 'good' and 'bad', as though they were universal truths. For example, they might say "You're lazy if you don't do anything," or, "It's rude to ask questions." When values are passed on in this way children are given the impression that there are objective standards to be lived up to. When adults say something like, "Don't shout; it's naughty," their own need for peace and quiet - their half of the equation - remains unacknowledged. It is more helpful to a noisy child if the adult says "I can't handle your shouting. Would you go and shout somewhere else." This brings about the goal of peace for the adult in a positive way without implying criticism of the child's behaviour. Quite clearly shouting is not naughty; sometimes it is appropriate or even vital in an emergency situation. When adults acknowledge their own needs and limitations a child can develop a realistic way of behaving with standards of behaviour that are personal and do not pretend to be universal.

When children begin to exercise their will-power or their desire to explore and express themselves, they begin to mistrust their impulses towards self-expression if they are controlled with shame or blame. "Don't be greedy," or, "Stop being silly," teaches them to be ashamed of their impulses and to expect criticism whenever they express their feelings or their individuality. Instead of receiving guidance towards mature and considerate self-expression, they are confronted with two alternatives, either to stop behaving in the way that is disapproved of and to conform, or to continue and be seen as rebellious or 'bad'. Furthermore, when children are told repeatedly that they are silly or selfish, etc. they begin to believe that these characteristics are part of their personality. If no distinction is made between who the child is and what she does, the *child* will feel that she is rejected, rather than that the behaviour is inappropriate in a particular situation.

Carl Rogers suggests that information received in this way from adults leads to the formation of 'introjected values' which are beliefs and perceptions we have about ourselves such as, "I am stupid,"....."I am clumsy,"....."I can't do things," or "I can't trust myself." These come from the unquestioned adoption of outside values formed at a time when we were too young to do anything other than believe what we were told, too young to check out the 'truth' against our own experience of ourselves. Personal values learnt through shame and blame produce attitudes like, "People will be looking for my faults,"....."I can't trust others," or "It's bad to ask for what you want." When values are not owned as personal, children grow into adults who find it difficult to accept differences in others and who will expect to control others by criticism and matching them up to a bogus set of behaviour 'rules'.

Most of us have beliefs like these about ourselves, which seem to us to be as true as if they were born out of our own experience, but which, in actuality reflect the way adults moulded us when we were young. We carry them around with us in adult life and continue the process that our parents and teachers started. We need constantly to justify our behaviour in order to protect ourselves from the ever present threat of criticism. We allow the voice in our head that says, "Keep quiet, people will think you're showing off," or "It's no good, I can't change anything," to control our actions. There are times when it is sensible to *choose* these responses, but when we operate from introjected values it is as if they are always true for every situation. If we do not challenge these introjected values we are destined to repeat the same familiar patterns over and over again, and limit ourselves like a workman who uses the same few tools for a range of different jobs, regardless of whether they are appropriate or not.

In training
Ask Yourself:
What introjected values do I have? In other words what things do I believe about myself, or others, that do not match up to reality? For example, "Untidy children aren't intelligent."

Our introjected values can distort the way we communicate with others too; we learn that it is safer to manipulate people for what we want, rather than ask directly. For example, imagine a situation when two teachers do break-duty together. One of them would like to skip the duty because they have some last-minute preparation to do for their next lesson. If they are influenced by the introjected value that says, "It's selfish to ask for what you want," they will feel safer trying to 'engineer' it rather than to come right out and ask. Instead of asking their partner whether they could manage alone and offering to negotiate some kind of compromise, they feel guilty. And so they might do the duty reluctantly and spend the time complaining about their work load until *their partner* suggests they go off and finish their preparation. Or they might 'forget' to turn up or spend the entire duty being bad-tempered with children. Meanwhile, their partner, if influenced by their own introjected value thinks, "I must put the needs of others before my own," or, "I mustn't say 'No'," is either manipulated into doing the duty alone or feels puzzled and uncomfortable, and unable to do anything about these feelings.

In Training
Share times when you have experienced being manipulated. How did you feel about it?

Contd. In pairs try to get your partner to do something for you without asking them directly. Then ask them directly to do something. Talk about the different feelings involved in both scenarios, and on both the 'asked' and the 'asking' side.

Being controlled by shame and blame leads us to confuse what is good for us with what is socially acceptable. We tie ourselves up in a web of 'oughts' and 'shoulds' that are not always in our best interests. We lack confidence in our own judgement and our freedom of action is limited, because we've not had the space in the past to learn from our mistakes or to be ourselves and to accept the consequences of that.

Hidden motivations
We can increase our awareness of the way communications are affected by introjected values and the feelings they evoke, by exploring the *processes* underlying communication. When we communicate we use much more than words to convey our message, for example, body language, facial expression and tone of voice are influenced by our introjects. Very often we are unaware of some of the non-verbal messages we are giving out and receiving; yet they have as much, if not more, influence on the outcome of an interaction as the words. Yet in daily life, most of our attention focuses on the content, or the words and overt actions of an interaction, rather than the process, or the underlying intention.

Imagine three children on their lunch-break: one is making a paper aeroplane, another is sitting reading a magazine and a third comes along and starts talking. The overt actions and words of the three form the content that we tend to focus upon. The process of what is going on, in contrast, lies in the way these children feel whilst they are folding, reading and talking and the way these feelings affect their communications and behaviour. The reader might be totally absorbed or merely flicking through the magazine, their mind occupied somewhere else. The person making the paper plane might be feeling satisfied or frustrated, happy to be with the others, or wishing they would go away. The talker might feel confident and sure of her welcome or tentative because she fears rejection. All these feelings have a crucial effect on the outcome of any interaction that takes place between these three young people, yet they go largely unrecognised and unacknowledged.

If the talker feels elated because she has just scored points in a basket ball game, it is unlikely that she could express this elation comfortably without provoking some kind of reaction in the others based on their feelings about success and failure. If the person making the plane has internalised the 'rule' that talking about your success is only done by people who are big-headed they will not react kindly to the girl, who could end up feeling hurt or put down for no reason that she can understand because she doesn't know the other's hidden feelings about success.

It is essential to be aware of the influence of our internal world on the way we interact with others. An internal world made up of rules, beliefs, labels and events which shape and limit our perceptions of what is acceptable, possible and likely to happen. We not only need to acknowledge this process, but also to take responsibility for it, and develop ways of expressing it consciously and positively. To be able to do this we need to feel safe enough to examine our inner values and change them as our needs change and as our daily experience questions their validity and appropriateness. Feedback from others is an essential element in this self-knowledge process.

The Core Conditions

Carl Rogers realised that a particular set of circumstances is necessary for someone to feel safe enough to acknowledge and explore their introjected values and to be themselves. These circumstances have come to be called the Core Conditions and Rogers states that without them, positive change or self-development cannot take place. As well as being *necessary* they are also *sufficient*, in other words, the experience of the core conditions alone is sufficient to engender change in those who want to do so. Briefly the core conditions are empathy, warmth and genuineness.

Such conditions are useful for teachers who want to create a climate of trust for their pupils so that effective communication and personal development can take place. Indeed, *any* interaction between people will benefit from an attempt to be genuine, warm and empathic.

Empathy

Being empathic requires a certain amount of self-reflection and an awareness and understanding of the way in which we relate to others. Firstly, we need to be able to agree that no one person can experience objective reality or the 'whole truth'. Everything is relative; what one person means by 'cold' or 'good' or 'naughty' will not necessarily correspond to someone else's understanding of the same words. When teachers, for example, are trying to agree on standards of behaviour for their pupils, they may well all have a quite different definition of what constitutes 'unacceptable'. In this situation, it is more constructive if they try to understand each other and come to some kind of agreement, rather than try to convince the other person that their definition is 'wrong', because who knows the 'right' definition anyway?

Empathy means trying to understand others, by trying to see the world as they see it and communicating this fact by 'active listening'. Carl Rogers placed particular emphasis on being able accurately and sensitively to understand another's feelings *without getting them muddled up with your own.* He made it clear that we cannot actually put ourselves into the world of others. Even if we have similar experiences, we will not have felt the same about it.

Genuineness

The second core condition is that of genuineness, which means being able to be honest about the way you're feeling and, where appropriate, to give this information to the people you're with; rather than acting the part of the person who can handle everything or the aloof professional, authority figure who keeps their feelings to themselves. This means that we bring our whole selves to our relationships; our feelings, thoughts and attitudes, 'warts and all'. Again, this isn't easy. My training as a teacher created in me the assumption that I am supposed know all the answers. I had an image of what a teacher is supposed to be like and tried to live up to it. Part of my image of 'the perfect teacher' was that it is inappropriate for a teacher to show their real feelings. But unacknowledged feelings often have the nasty habit of leaking out anyway, leaving those around you, and perhaps yourself too, feeling confused and hurt. It is useful if teachers can admit to feeling unsure of something or to feeling sad because their cat has died, or repulsed by the smell of sweaty feet! It was a relief to me when I realised that I was not the only one responsible for what went on in my classroom. Everyone plays a part in the equation, if there is an acknowledgement that feelings, feelings of all the people present, influence situations then the responsibility of what happens in a given situation lies with everyone present. A disastrous lesson is not just the teacher's fault. If we can admit to our feelings, own them, then we will give pupils permission to do the same.

Warmth

The final core condition is non-judgemental warmth, respect or 'unconditional positive regard'. Warmth is about being positive towards others, freeing them from our judgements, welcoming them, their differences and the particular qualities they bring to a situation. To be experienced as warm we need to display a caring respect for others, allowing them to be themselves and overcoming the temptation we often have to criticise their behaviour or suggest we know a better way for them to tackle things. It means having respect for the *person,* not judging them, no matter how much we dislike their behaviour, separating the behaviour of which we disapprove from the value of the person.   Our respect is not conditional upon 'correct behaviour', but neither does it mean that we have to condone unacceptable behaviour.   By making a distinction between what someone does and who they are it is possible to show warmth at the same time as setting boundaries, and expressing different opinions and wishes.

An example of a short conversation with a teenage boy might help to illustrate the core conditions.

> Teacher : How are you doing?
> Pupil : I had an argument with my mother, that's it really.
> T : You had an argument with your mum? You look really unhappy about it.
> P : Yes, we argued and that's all there is to say. But I can't stop thinking about it.
> T : So you don't feel that there is any point in talking about it but it's on your mind. Do you want to tell me what keeps going round your head?
> P : Well, I was watching TV and she bombed at me. So I got angry and shouted back.
> T : You look really sad about that.
> P : Yes I am. My Mum's solid. She always takes care of us. I don't think sons should shout at their mums.
> T : You love your mum, you don't like shouting at her, yet sometimes you get angry.
> P : Yes, that's it.
> T : Have you ever thought of telling your mum how you feel?

At this point he stopped, thought for a while, then his depressed expression lifted. He had found a way of putting things right, that he had some power to change things. He decided to tell his mum that evening. I found this conversation particularly interesting because at the beginning I assumed that this boy, like most of the young people I work with, would feel unfairly treated when his mother shouted at him for no reason. If I had followed this mistaken assumption, rather than the boy's words and feelings, he wouldn't have been able to find his resolution.

Carl Rogers used the core conditions as the basis of his psychotherapy with clients, but for them to be beneficial they have to be more than just *there*, they also have to be *experienced* by the client. In order for this to happen therapists developed specific skills to convey the core conditions. An understanding of counselling skills and person-centredness can empower you as well as the children you teach. Having counselling skills in your teaching 'tool box' will enhance all your interpersonal interactions. Creating an environment where the core conditions are important will give teachers back a feeling of control in their work and their lives and will substantially change the atmosphere of any school.

Counselling Skills   3

The core conditions are qualities; counselling skills are a way of communicating these qualities to other people. In some senses counselling skills are nothing out of the ordinary, they are things we can all do, and probably do do to varying degrees. Sometimes all we need to do is to use the skills we already have consciously and with the intention of being person-centred.

Listening

When my son was due to go up to his second class after the summer holidays, it was obvious to me that he was unhappy about it. I thought he was nervous about having a new teacher, but although I tried to convince him she was really nice, it had no effect. As the start of the new term got closer, I was beginning to dread the idea of him going to school crying. I was tempted to tell him to pull himself together and not to make such a fuss. Instead, I made a determined attempt to listen to what he was trying to tell me. Eventually, I found out that he had the idea that he was the *only* one moving up. I was able to explain what was really going to happen and he went off to school quite happily. My assumptions were wrong, and trying to talk him out of his feelings did not work. Although listening takes more time and patience initially, it saves a lot of trouble in the end!

Good listening is not necessarily an ability that we are born with. It is a skill that can be learnt and passed on to others. Whether you are teaching or having a conversation, listening, and communicating this fact to your pupils and colleagues, is a way of showing that you are being empathic and warm. Pupils learn from being listened to and will start to use listening skills for themselves. I have learnt from my experience both as a counsellor and a client that when people try to communicate, their first concern is to be understood and believed. This is especially important for children because they cannot always express themselves clearly. Adults do not always take the time to listen to a child or give them the same respect as they would another adult, especially if what they are saying seems to rock the boat or the speaker is struggling to express themselves. If we do not have respect for what children say, it is hard for them to develop their self-respect and a confidence in their ability to express themselves. I remember realising this for myself when I was in the sixth form when I was supposed to volunteer my views during time set aside for discussion. Up until then, experience had taught me that offering my opinion was a risky thing to do. I had not only stopped doing it, I was by that time too confused to know what to say for the best. Being open with teachers about my thoughts and feelings, I ran the risk of being called cheeky, stupid or awkward. I used my energy to try to work out what they wanted to hear, or what would wind them up, but either way an opportunity for a step towards maturity was denied me at that time.

Making space
The first requirement of good listening is to give people your time. Whether someone is answering a question in the middle of a busy lesson, or telling you a problem before class starts, hurrying them along will give them the impression that you don't value what they have to say, or that what they have to say is not worth hearing and by implication that they are worthless too. By giving your undivided attention, children feel valued. In order to do this you must, wherever possible, put aside your own preoccupations. If you are in a hurry be honest about it. Listening with half an ear does not fool anyone,

they know they are being short-changed! "I am interested in what you are saying but I have too much on my mind at the moment. Can we talk about it at break?" Or if the child needs longer than a few moments, then their need to talk should be treated seriously so it would help if you could find somewhere to talk undisturbed.

Put aside assumptions
It is important, too, when listening, to put aside your assumptions. Even if it is the fourth time someone has told you they've forgotten to do their homework, it is worth spending the time exploring what is going on, without jumping to conclusions or telling them how you feel about it and them. By taking time to explore, you will often find a pattern to the behaviour, and how it can be changed. Each child is different: your assumptions are rarely an accurate guide to what is happening. Cast your mind back to the first time you met a particular class of children and check the accuracy of the initial assumptions you made about them. "She's sitting alone; she must be quiet and shy. His work is untidy, he must be lazy." We take impressions in so quickly that we tend to think in stereotypes. There is nothing wrong with this, it helps us to make sense of the world a little at a time. However we do need to be aware of what we are doing. Individuals are complicated, and unrevised stereotypes have a habit of becoming self-fulfilling prophecies. Being a good judge of character can be useful, but always be open to the fact that it is possible that you can be mistaken.

In training
Go round the group. Try and guess what kind of house each person was brought up in. Share your guesses with the group, but don't correct each other's guesses. What did it feel like guessing without knowing if you were accurate or not. Share your responses to the guesses made about you.

Benefits of listening

If you take children seriously, by listening in order to understand what they have said sympathetically, they are more likely to respond to you with honesty - even if they started out with the intention of fobbing you off with an excuse! Children are not going to risk telling you the truth unless they trust you to be able to handle it and not use it to punish them. "I've lost my purse." "What did you do that for?" was what my mum would say, as if I'd done it on purpose. Like most of us, I learned to say as little as possible, or even to lie, in situations where I was likely to cop it. Good listening encourages trust and respect. *It is a way of showing warmth.*

Training Box
Working in small groups, come up with some memories about the kind of listening you experienced as a child, at school and at home. Identify the qualities of a good listener and the benefits to people. Share these with the group.

When thinking about listening, it is important to keep a sense of perspective. I am not suggesting that you need to give your complete attention every time a child talks to you. This is neither practical nor necessary; teachers need to develop a range of skills and select which one is appropriate. Some children just like to chatter for the pleasure of playing with words. More often than not, in this case, all they require is a feeling of trust. But there are also times when talking is inappropriate and children need to learn to be silent and listen!

Encouraging

If you have the time and space to listen to what someone is saying to you there are ways to let them know that you are listening. Firstly there is body language. If you have ever been listened to by someone who keeps looking at someone else, makes no response to what you are saying, or who is frowning, you will know that you quickly dry up and start wishing that you had never begun. The same applies to someone who looks unblinkingly into your eyes without a break. Whilst someone is talking to you, an occasional encouraging nod lets them know you are following what they are saying. Verbal encouragement can take the form of "Go on, I see, Mm." Allowing the child to fall silent conveys patience and warmth and when you do speak, a calm unhurried voice has a reassuring effect on the child.

In training
1. Get into pairs. One in each pair is asked to talk for a minute or two on a light topic such as their latest holiday. The other person is given instructions on how to listen badly. For example, they can look bored, ask irrelevant questions, jump to conclusions, be preoccupied with something else. Feed back to the group how it felt to be listened to badly. Brainstorm how you recognise good and bad listening.
2. Divide into pairs and listen attentively and encouragingly this time. Take turns to tell each other something that has happened to you recently (be careful what you choose, nothing too raw). Feed back to each other the responses that made you feel listened to. Group brainstorm on listening skills both verbal and non-verbal.

Reflective listening

When people speak to us we need to accept what they say as a statement of how they feel, instead of trying to talk them out of it as we are sometimes tempted to do. As in, "I'm really fed up." "Fed up? You shouldn't be fed up at your age!" Other times we pick up on the bit that interests us most, like, "I'm tired because the baby wakes me at night." "Oh, you didn't tell me you had a new baby in the family. Is it a boy or girl?" We may compete with the speaker, "*I'm* not scared of flying," or be tempted to be judgmental, "Don't be so silly." None of these responses tries to understand the speaker or really hears what they are saying, they are not being empathic or respectful.

Reflective listening is listening with the sole purpose of understanding what someone is saying, in the same way you listen when you are being given directions or instructions. That is, repeating back the essentials of what you have been told, in your own words so that you can convey and check that you have understood. If you get it wrong first time, it doesn't matter. In allowing the speaker to correct you, you are helping them to clarify their thoughts and feelings.

The aim of reflective listening is to act like a mirror and reflect back verbally, without judgement or bias, what you see in order to give the speaker the knowledge that they are understood or at least that you are making an effort to understand them. It also gives them the opportunity to hear their own words and feelings spoken and understood by someone else, often to very powerful effect.

In training
Divide into pairs. Take turns to speak about yourselves for a minute or two. Then repeat your partner's words to the group. What was it like to hear your words being spoken by someone else. If they got things wrong how did you feel about being misinterpreted? If, when it was your turn to talk, you got something wrong, how did it feel to be corrected?

It is especially useful if, when reflecting back, you include any feelings shown by the speaker. Sometimes people convey their feelings in body language and facial expression, and are hardly aware of this. All too often we ignore the 'feeling content' of a message. Sometimes we reject feelings by trying to talk people out of them, because we cannot handle them - "Don't cry. Cheer up." It is often a relief to people when their feelings are acknowledged, because it means their feeling have been accepted; "You looked really upset when you said that. Were you upset?" However, in acknowledging feelings, you need to allow the child to correct you if your observation was inaccurate. Otherwise they can feel as though they are being 'told' how to feel. It is also important that your voice sounds concerned rather than judgmental. If the person feels criticised you can trigger a defence, "Me? I'm not upset!" or, "Well *you* would be upset too!" Reflective listening is crucial in conveying the core condition of empathy. Of course it would sound stilted simply to reflect back ad infinitum whenever anyone talked to you. But it is worth taking the time to check that you have understood the content and acknowledge important feelings, before responding to a speaker.

In training

1. In pairs take it in turns to talk briefly about something you have some strong feelings about; something that makes you happy, angry, sad, fearful, etc. The other one of the pair to try to identify the feeling and how they recognised it.

2. Either split into twos to discuss and identify any feelings that you find hard to handle or spend some time thinking about them for yourself.

Responding

When you are sure that you have understood what is being said, it is useful to refer to the core conditions when you reply. Whether you are responding to, or asking, a question, trying to sort out a problem, holding a conversation, or teaching, the words you use and the way you use them will carry a message which provokes a particular response. And some responses are less helpful than others.

Giving advice

When responding, whether during a conversation or whilst teaching, giving advice is a tricky business, it can lead to the "Yes but...." syndrome which could go on for ever like the 'Hole in My Bucket' song!

"I'm late because I haven't got an alarm clock."

"Well, you should buy one."

"Yes but I haven't got any money."

"You should get a Saturday job."

"Yes, but then I'd not have the time to do my homework." etc.

This results in feelings of frustration on both sides. If the recipient does not feel able to follow the advice, he either makes excuses, feels obliged to accept it, tries to follow the advice and fails or feels bossed about and misunderstood. Telling someone what to do rarely solves a problem unless the advice has been requested. If you do have some advice or information to give to someone, before giving it, ask them if they want to hear it. "I've got some ideas about being late. Do you want to hear them?" When giving advice words like 'ought' and 'should' are more likely to trigger a negative response. Advice in the form of suggestions is less likely to be interpreted as telling someone what to do, because it allows the recipient some control and choice, "Perhaps you could buy an alarm clock. Do you think that would help?"

> In training
> Outline a problem (real or imaginary) to the group, members of the group to respond by telling you what they would do if they had the same problem. Report back to the group how that felt. Then explore the same problem with open-ended questions and suggestions. Compare this experience to the first one.

Questions
There are many reasons for asking questions but they fall into two broad categories; inviting the expression of feelings and opinions or eliciting a specific piece of information. There are also, basically two types of questions; closed questions, which are a way of narrowing down the field or pinning someone down to a direct,

specific answer such as "When are you going to buy an alarm clock?" and open-ended questions which invite exploration. For example an open-ended question to the latecomer could be, "What can we do about that?" or "How can you get to school on time without an alarm clock?" Whichever kind of question you are asking, your tone of voice often has more impact than the words. "How are you going to get to school on time?" can be experienced either as a pinning down or an invitation to exploration depending on whether it is spoken in a warm caring way or a challenging way.

In training
In small groups, think back to your own schooling, the way you were questioned and how you felt about it. Brainstorm different types of questions with examples. Think of as many reasons as possible for asking these questions. How would you personally respond to being asked some of these questions? Are there some circumstances when they would be OK, or when might they not be?

In asking a question it is important to be aware of the reason you are asking it. Do you want to elicit a particular answer or to establish whether they know a particular piece of information or are you trying to find out their opinion? Is asking a question the most appropriate way of achieving your objective? Teachers ask a lot of questions and most of them are closed or recall questions. Recall questions are useful in finding out what children already know, getting them to recount personal experiences or give descriptions. They are also particularly useful with younger children for breaking the ice, e.g. "Where do you live? What's you name?" etc. However, recall questions inhibit discussion and restrict participation. The flow of communication is manipulated by the questioner. When in doubt, children are unlikely to make a guess at answering a recall question because, if they get it wrong they might look foolish or evoke a critical response. For example, I once saw a training video where the teacher asked the class, "Why is today a special day?" The children knew that she was expecting one particular answer, some of them did not know what the answer was, which ruled them out of the discussion. Others made a guess and got it wrong. Even some of the children who got the right answer did not particularly think of the day as special. The flow of communication was inhibited by this question. If a teacher is hoping for a discussion, it is more productive to make a statement and invite responses. "Today is a special day to me, because it is St Patrick's Day. Could you tell me about your special day?" This allows the children space to respond to her statement and to volunteer their own views.

In conversations, interviews or during class teaching, open-ended questions encourage the flow of discussion. They also encourage trust because speakers are helped to come up with a response from their own experience, rather than being led by the nose to a predetermined answer. Open-ended questions are an important way of showing respect and developing confidence, in effect you are saying, "I value you because I want to know your opinion."

Response times
Generally, teachers do not wait long enough for responses to their questions and statements. When the wait-time is increased by just a few seconds there are several beneficial effects. More children participate, their answers are more considered and their confidence to speculate increases. They are also more likely to ask their own questions and discuss ideas amongst themselves. When anyone is given more time to consider their response, they are more likely to give something of themselves.

Dealing with difficult things
However skilful a communicator you are, there will be times when a child tells you something that you have difficulty in dealing with. With the best of intentions there will always be children who can

'press one of your buttons' so that you feel angry or upset, they may touch on a subject you know little about, or a subject you feel uncomfortable with or unqualified to talk about. In these instances, be genuine, "I'm too angry to talk now, I need some time to think," or, "I don't know enough about it; shall I try to find someone who does?" This is better than trying to help regardless, because your discomfort will show and could be interpreted by the child (or colleague) as disapproval or disinterest.

There may even be an occasion when a child tells you something where, for your own professional safety, you will need to pass on the information to the Head, police or parents.

In training
Make a list of things you would have difficulty coping with if a child brought them to you.
In a group discuss the sort of things that you would need to seek help from somebody else, for your own or the child's protection. Check the school's policy on some of the more sensitive issues of confidentiality and your legal requirement. What are your own views on confidentiality?

More about the core conditions

To help to consolidate the theory of the core conditions and the skills which you can use to communicate them, here are some examples of the way they have been useful to me as a teacher.

Empathy

Discussions generally proceed on the assumption that, if there are differing points of view, only one person can be 'right'. Politicians are adept at this kind of logical arguments. Rather than try to understand someone else's opposing point of view, they try to prove it 'wrong'. Yet, we all experience reality in a different way and there is seldom an objective, unassailable position in any discussion. Each person's point of view is useful. A more constructive approach to differing view points is to accept that each person's experience is true *for them*. Understanding someone else's world, putting yourself in their shoes, and respecting their right to their opinion, is empathy.

When pupils used to tell me that they hated school, I would try and talk them out if it and persuade them that they needed an education. However, my response did not improve their school attendance. It either evoked a polite agreement to shut me up, or a rebellious argument.

Empathy does not mean that you have to agree with everything someone tells you. I still believe that getting an education is important, but I now appreciate that my pupils are not necessarily going to feel the same way as I do. I try to understand their feelings about school and give them some space to explore them. "You really hate school, don't you. And you seem angry and upset when you talk about it." When they feel that their feelings are accepted as valid, they no longer need to 'defend their corner'. Which means that they are more likely to take responsibility for themselves, because the choice is theirs. "Well I know I need an education if I want to get a job," or "Being at school makes me feel stupid, I'd rather not put myself through that." There is more scope for honesty and change on both sides.

In training
In pairs. Choose someone who you know well and who knows you well; your mother, brother, best friend, etc. Imagine yourself to be that person and now you are going to talk about yourself from that person's point of view and your partner is going to ask you questions yourself. To make this clearer, if Judith and Mary are doing this exercise together..........contd...

Contd.....Judith may choose to be her best friend, Jane. Jane is now going, with the help of questions from Mary, to talk about Judith. Mary can ask questions like, "What are Judith's good points?" "How do you feel about Judith?" "What are her weak points?" When you have done this for a few minutes share what it felt like to be in the shoes of someone else and to hear what they had to say about you. Swap roles.

Warmth

A child who experiences warmth, or 'unconditional positive regard' will grow up much better able to cope with stress and problems than one who does not. To give warmth means to accept and respect another person. You show warmth whenever you convey to another person that they are worthwhile and important. As when you are pleased to see them, give them your time and are positive about their behaviour. People tend to make the warmth they give conditional on the behaviour of others. When this happens to children they are given the message "I will only care about you if you behave the way I want you to behave, and be the kind of person I approve of. Otherwise you don't have any worth." If caring is unconditional, the child is free to make their own decisions and consequently take responsibility for them.

I used to get confused when the young people I taught told me about their criminal offences. I did not want to condone violent behaviour or theft, yet I wanted to work with them in a constructive and warm way. By separating what they do from who they are, I am able to relate to them more effectively. I can be pleased to see them, point out their strengths and care about their welfare. I can also confront them about their offences.

In training
1. In pairs share the times in your childhood when you experienced warmth at school and the times when you didn't.
2. As a group brainstorm ways of showing warmth in school. Write them up on a flip chart.

Genuineness

To be genuine means to be yourself and to operate from your own feelings and experience rather than to act the part of the professional. When I started teaching there were times when I was unsure of how I was supposed to be with children. How much familiarity to tolerate, how to respond to their affection or their cheekiness. When we had visitors, I would imagine them judging me as either too progressive or too much the opposite. It took me some time to realise that I was alright the way I was, with my own standards of behaviour. By identifying the behaviour I felt comfortable with and the standards I regarded as important, my objectives became clearer. There are times when, as a member of an institution, you may have to uphold standards that are not your own. In this case I have found the truth a more effective way of getting co-operation. "Maybe school uniform isn't a good idea, but I have to obey rules too and insist that you wear it," or "I don't want to risk getting into trouble by letting you out of school in lesson time."

When considering expressing your feelings it is important to know that you need to be selective about what you reveal and how you reveal it. Either in day to day interactions or in specific instances when someone has come to you to talk about something that is troubling them you should only reveal that about yourself which is appropriate or helpful to them, and that does not switch the focus of the interaction away from them and onto you. In two-way conversations between peers, the focus of attention normally swings from one to the other unless one has a particular need to be the centre, but if your help is being sought you will have to put your needs aside for the time being and then seek help elsewhere if you need to. If a child, for example, is telling you about their mother who is ill in hospital it would be inappropriate for you to burst into tears because it reminds you of your own parent's illness. You may be genuinely sad but to act out that sadness there and then would be unhelpful. It may be good to acknowledge your feelings but keep the focus on them, "What you've been talking about reminds me of when my Mum was ill and I feel sad again, but please continue." If have the feelings and don't acknowledge them the other person may sense and wrongly interpret your behaviour. So it's a fine, and sometimes difficult balance between revelations and silences.

****

If you decide to change the way you are communicating with your pupils, it will take some time for you to effect this change and for them to get the message that things are different. But knowing about counselling skills and using them to inform your interpersonal relationships will be a good starting point.

Summaries

Listening
- give your full attention
- make space - at another time if necessary
- don't jump to conclusions
- let them tell you rather than make assumptions
- believe the speaker.

Encouraging
show that you are listening by:
- setting aside enough time
- encouraging body language
- encouraging verbal cues and tone of voice.

Reflective listening
- mirror back what you have 'received' by summarising the speaker's words and feelings
- seek confirmation that you have understood by checking your understanding with the speaker
- be prepared to be corrected - it is important to get it right.

Responding
Offering advice
- try to avoid giving advice as your first option
  ask before giving advice
- make suggestions rather than telling someone what to do
- avoid words like 'ought' and 'should'.

Questions
- don't ask too many questions
- don't ask questions just to fill gaps
- choose the kind of question that achieves your goal e.g:
  - open questions and statements encourage communication
  - closed questions narrow the field
  - recall questions elicit information

Waiting
- increase the time you wait for a response
- don't be tempted to fill a long silence, the talker may appreciate the space
- take time to consider your responses

The Core Conditions
Empathy
- try to understand the world of the other person *as they experience it*
- accept their point of view as having equal validity
- don't confuse your feelings with theirs and vice versa

Warmth
- be positive and welcoming
- give your time
- separate who people are from what they do
- believe the speaker
- trust them to find their own solution
- remember their right to do what they choose, even if you disagree

Genuineness
- be yourself, be real
- but reveal only that about yourself that is to the benefit of the person who is talking to you
- don't hide behind the role of the 'professional'

More Skills **4**

Communication skills

Teachers know all about the importance of being able to communicate well as an essential teaching tool. The skills of communication include being able to talk at an appropriate level for the age and ability of pupils in an interesting, knowledgeable and engaging way are what most teachers are well used to using but there are more skills in communication that are not seen as so obviously necessary.

The communication skills of negotiating, giving and receiving feedback, assertiveness and conflict management are equally crucial to teachers. They are different from counselling skills but can be instrumental in providing the core conditions and are generally learnt in a person-centred, experiential way. Whilst counselling skills help to create a warm environment, teachers do have to do more than communicate their ability to listen and respond to their pupils. They have to manage children and motivate them to do things, discuss opinions and give advice. These skills apply equally to staff management and relationships between colleagues.

When you train in communication skills you develop an understanding of the communication process, identify the situations which you experience as stressful and practise strategies for dealing with them.

Using communication skills does not guarantee peace and harmony; someone determined to have an argument will generally find a way of provoking one. However, if conflict happens, you can learn how to avoid contributing to it and to develop a wider range of skills for dealing with it constructively.

Managing pupil behaviour

When I trained as a teacher, in the sixties, the predominant philosophy then seemed to be that children's behaviour was determined by the quality of the teacher's lessons. Having been neatly ascribed behaviour problems to boredom, the origins and processes of interpersonal conflicts that occur in schools were never discussed in their own right. The subject of keeping order in a class was a bit like death, something you weren't encouraged to talk about. And if you broke the taboo, you lay yourself open to the charge of inadequacy or being ill-prepared; the implication being, that if you're a good teacher you'll have no problems. Which to some extent is true; but it's not as easy as that; even teachers with good interpersonal skills find things difficult sometimes.

When I started teaching, I felt as though I had been thrown in at the deep end. Whilst interesting and relevant teaching materials were, of course, important, I would get into countless battles every day. Many of these had the potential for escalating into major conflicts ranging from petty arguments about equipment to wrangles about behaviour both inside and outside the classroom. Learning to manage pupil behaviour by trial and error was exhausting, stressful and very inefficient. I felt as though I was having to re-invent the wheel every day.

In training
Share some of the behaviour of pupils that you have difficulty coping with. What behaviour of yours did your teachers find difficult?

Conflict

Conflict is a major source of problems. It exists in all creative situations because we are all different and therefore have different agendas. If you feel threatened by conflict, strong emotions such as fear, guilt and anger will arise. Feelings about conflict influence the way you respond to it.

Basically there are five reasons for conflict - differences of interests, values, styles (ways of doing things), opinions and understanding. By recognising the type of conflict you are experiencing, you can begin to move towards managing conflict rather than just reacting to it.

In training
Make your own definition of conflict. Group brainstorm the situations where conflict can arise in school. What does it mean to you? How do you feel when it happens? How does it come up for you in school?

I can remember an instance when simply asking a child to take his hat off provoked a chain of events that escalated out of all proportion to the original incident. I was never sure exactly how it happened, it was all so quick and once started impossible to stop. On reflection, I realised that the hat wasn't worth all the trouble, but nevertheless I still needed to feel I had some control. By interpreting this conflict as a challenge to my authority and therefore getting myself into the situation where I needed to win, I was making things difficult for myself! To lose the battle, by letting the child keep his hat on, seemed like failure, but then so did the alternative of taking the child to the Head!

The way we respond to conflict reflects our inner feelings of self-worth. If we feel that a child is deliberately trying to challenge our authority or that conflict is a sign of failure on our part, we can lose sight of the actual difference of opinion the triggered off the argument in the first place.

The way we send and receive messages establishes a climate for our relationships. If your messages are influenced by 'oughts' and 'shoulds' and feelings of failure, the difference between you and the child is more likely to escalate into an argument, a win/lose situation.

In training
Brainstorm conflict-provoking behaviour in teachers and pupils. (Use you memories of being at school as a pupil, as well as your current experience as a teacher) What feelings do they produce? What are the good feelings that could come from conflict? There are no right answers here.

Conflict contains the potential for resolution as well as destruction. By managing conflict rather than reacting to it, we can come out of it feeling good and turning it to good account. To achieve this goal, we need to be able to spot the situations where conflict can arise and then give ourselves the time to slow down and think of a way to respond positively rather than get swept along with the strong feelings. If you understand and respect differences of outlook, you are less likely to feel threatened by them. You can look for a way of negotiating a solution that you both feel good about, a win/win result rather than a win/lose outcome.

There are three ways of responding to differences; passively, aggressively or assertively.

In training
Brainstorm passive and aggressive actions and words that are responses to conflict.

Assertiveness

When we need to ask someone to do something for us or to give us something we need, we can ask aggressively, passively or assertively. Putting it crudely, aggressive people try to compel someone to give them what they want by coercion, shouting, bullying, intimidating, threatening or blaming. Passive people hope they will get what they want, apologising for wanting it, or get someone else to ask for them. Those who are assertive, are able to express their wishes, opinions and feelings in a relaxed, open way, confident that they have the right to ask, whilst, at the same time, respecting the rights of the other person.

Some people shy away from the idea of being assertive because they have the idea that it is the same as being aggressive. However, if you work with people, you cannot avoid expressing your own needs. Assertiveness acknowledges the fact that in any relationship, you have to express your needs or wants and that this can be done in a way that does not bring success to one person at the expense of the other.

The aim of assertiveness training is to help people to develop their confidence, so that they feel comfortable when asking for what they want, and can express themselves without being manipulative or overpowering. At the same time, it is also very much about respecting the rights of the other person; their right to ask *you* for what *they* want in return or even to refuse your request. Assertive people are less likely to feel threatened by the idea of someone challenging them. If it happens - and it will - they know that they can deal with it and even use it constructively.

In training
How do you respond to aggressive, passive and assertive people?

Why do we need to learn assertiveness?

You only have to listen to a small child asking for an ice-cream to know that we all instinctively know how to ask for what we want. But by the time we are out of the nursery, most of us have lost it, or rather, we have had it gradually shamed out of us by adults who can't handle their child's willpower. We are taught that "He who asks doesn't get," or we are praised for pleasing others and accused of being selfish if we try to please ourselves. We often end up thinking that there are no alternatives to either pleasing others or being aggressive in order to get what we want.

I am not suggesting that we should indulge a child's every whim but that it is the shame and blame that can be dispensed with. There is no need to blame someone for asking for what they want. We can teach children to respect the rights of others by setting an example. "Can I sit next to James?" "No, because the last time you sat next to him, you talked all lesson," is more constructive than, "You are far too naughty to choose who you can sit next to!" The shaming, blaming kind of response can be implied by the tone of voice as well as the words. We learn that it is safer to ask people for something by using shame and guilt and so it gets passed on by example from generation to generation. Being aggressive doesn't work either because people either do things grudgingly and you lose any future goodwill or they object to your manner and refuse out of principal to teach you a lesson or to punish you.

In order to become more assertive it is necessary to identify the situations that you want to change. When you start to try to change yourself, it is important to begin by changing your approach to the simplest and least threatening situations and to give yourself credit, or even a tangible reward, when you have achieved your goal. For example, I once worked with a child who really irritated me. It got to the stage where I could not see anything positive about him. I set myself the target of looking for something 'good' about his behaviour, praising him and welcoming him with a smile when he came into the room. When I succeeded in this target I bought myself a new pair of earrings!

In training
Ask yourself :-
Can you express your feelings, opinions and requests openly? Can you say "No," when you are asked to do something you don't want to do? Can you give and receive compliments? Who do you find yourself having most difficulty communicating with?

Knowing your rights

To be assertive you need to acknowledge that fact that, as a human being, you are entitled to certain rights. "I have a right to make my own decisions and take the consequences for them," or "I have a right to spend my money as I choose." You also have the right to state your needs. People may accept the right of others but can be less protective of their own rights. For example they allow others to change their minds or to make mistakes, but feel guilty when they do the same.

In training
Make a list of your own Bill of Rights: read them to a partner who should affirm each one as it is read, "Yes, you do have the right to change your mind." Feedback how it felt to the group. Identify your rights as a person, a teacher, an employee.

This process helps you to identify and establish your own standards rather than operate from standards imposed on you by others when you were too young to question them. It also gives insight into the ways in which you undermine yourself through guilt or ambivalence about whether you are entitled to ask for what you want or to behave in a particular way.

For example, in the 70s I worked in a school for young people in custody. The prison officers patrolling the school used to be critical if the inmates looked out of the windows during lessons, yet, because they spent most of their time in their cells, it was the best view they could get all week. When I started the job, I obviously didn't want to create the impression that I wasn't doing it properly. But I also wanted to be fair to the boys. So because I was ambivalent about where I stood on the matter, I found myself getting involved in daily arguments with my pupils. Eventually I realised that I had the right to protect my job, "If you look out of the window during the lesson, I run the risk of losing my job. From now on you can only look out of the window at the end of the lesson, when you have finished your work." They seemed to find this acceptable. It is important in a classroom that everyone knows exactly what is expected of them, and what will happen if the rules are broken.

In training
Working in pairs make a list of the rights of teachers and pupils in the classroom and what you can do if they are infringed. Be creative!

Being positive

Assertiveness is not just a skill to use when dealing with negative situations, it is also a positive way of relating to others and evaluating your lifestyle. If you are comfortable with the idea that no-one is perfect, you are less critical of yourself, and others, if mistakes are made. This means that you can allow yourself to take the risk of initiating changes and actively seeking to improve your circumstances. We tend to put ourselves last in our list of priorities. Try putting yourself first for a change; you might decide to devote some energy to mending something that has been irritating you, or trying out a new way of behaving in a particular situation. Making a conscious effort to look for and comment on the good in others creates a positive change too, because those around us feel more confident and valued.

More assertiveness techniques

There are various strategies which help people protect themselves from being manipulated into an argument or from being coerced into doing something they don't actually want to do. These strategies work both ways because, by using them, you become less manipulative or coercive.

Fogging

Fogging is a way of responding to 'put downs' by ignoring the hidden blame in a statement and calmly answering only the meaning of the words, i.e. ignoring the process and responding only to the content. On being faced with, "Your class was noisy!" many of us would get stung into defensiveness by the implied disapproval. Then we would argue or feel frustrated with the other person. But "Yes, that's true, they were," takes the wind right out of their sails and prevents possible conflict or hurt feelings.

'Put downs' are ways of implying criticisms in order to make others feel small or to manipulate them into doing something they do not want to do. These 'put downs' come in many forms; they can be disguised by a jokey tone of voice, "It's only a bit of fun," or "Can't you take a joke?" or they can be openly hostile as in "Here comes Wonder Boy." Being on the receiving end can result in feelings of hurt or anger.

> In training
> Brainstorm examples of different types of verbal and non-verbal 'put downs' and what they really imply, e.g. "Haven't you done the register *yet*?" - meaning "You're so lazy/disorganised." Share any put-downs you experience at school.

Another way of Fogging is called 'negative assertion', which means that you agree with the criticism, if it's true, but again, do not accept the implied blame or shame. For example, "Your class room is untidy," if you reply, "No, it isn't!" you are setting things up for an argument about standards by polarising yourself and the speaker on to different sides. The answer, "Yes, I am untidy sometimes," or "Well yes, it isn't as tidy as yours," acknowledges the truth of what is said, and ignores any implied criticism of your standards. If the other person was intending to put you down, they get little satisfaction from the exchange. However, if they were giving you constructive advice you can ask for more information, if you feel it is appropriate. "What kind of storage do you think would help?" This technique is also useful if you are inclined to hear criticism where none was intended!

In training
Brainstorm Fogging responses to the 'put downs' you identified in the exercise above. Practise fogging in pairs.

Fogging is useful too, when children try to put you down. "This is a baby game," answer with a smile, "Yes, it could have been too easy for you." Sometimes the child is trying to express a need for help whilst hanging on to their dignity, so you might say something like, "How can we make it more interesting?" Again, you are acknowledging the truth of the statement but not picking up the blame.

By being comfortable with the idea that you, like everyone, aren't perfect, people will have less scope for putting you down and get less satisfaction when they do it.

Broken record
For most of us it is difficult enough to ask for what we want once, but to continue asking for it if the person doesn't respond, is much worse. Maybe this is because we believe that we would be seen as nagging or pushy if we were to continue. Or perhaps it is because of the fear

of the further humiliation of being ignored. The technique called 'Broken record' is that of looking a person in the eye and persisting with your request! As children do when asking for an ice-cream. Vary your words a little but keep on asking, in a firm voice, for what you want. You may not always get it - nor should you - but keep on until you get what you want or a good reason why not. "I would like you to get on with your work." Just keep on asking. It helps if you ask in a voice that expects to be obeyed. Few children can ignore a broken record and I have found it especially useful after my third or fourth request, to look them straight in the eye and ask in a strong calm voice, "Are you going to disobey me?" Even if they were to say "Yes" - and no-one ever has - they have lost the battle to ignore me! It is also effective to add some empathy to the broken record, by recognising the other person's needs. "I can understand that you want to talk to Sharon, but I want you to get on with your work." Empathising with their wishes reduces the possibility of conflict. You are not criticising them for what they want to do, but asserting your rights as a teacher.

Negotiation skills

Assertiveness technique teaches us that you can ask someone to change what they are doing but not to change from being the kind of person they are. It also teaches us to be prepared to negotiate because other people have the right to say "No," to our request; we don't always want what is reasonable.

When you take an assertive approach to communication, you need to be open to the possibility of negotiation. As the word negotiation has become associated with industrial relations and court procedures, where both sides seem to be at loggerheads, people often think of it as a rather cold and legalistic way to approach relationships. However, if negotiation takes place in a climate of respect and honesty, it is a reasonable way of working out differences and meeting needs. Because principled negotiation respects the rights of both parties to have different needs, it opens up a way of responding creatively to the kind of issues that can cause conflict.

To negotiate assertively, you need to be able to take a step back from your negative feelings, to communicate what you want calmly and clearly and respect the other person's right to protect their own interests. If you can show warmth and empathy to a child, in a situation where you both have different priorities, you are not only giving him a good role model to take into adult life, but also as affirmation for his own sense of self-respect/worth. Negotiation is a constructive way of achieving goals.

Climate for negotiation
However, negotiation is not always the appropriate course of action: there are times when the difference isn't important enough to you, and also there are some things that are just not negotiable.

If you feel swept along in feelings of anger and frustration it is difficult to be positive and clear headed enough to negotiate on the spot. Sometimes, too, differences crop up when you are busy, or there are lots of other things happening. At these times, it is best to arrange to negotiate at some other time soon. There are some situations, too, where you feel that preparation might be necessary before you are ready to negotiate, such as finding out more information or clarifying your thoughts and feelings.

In training
When in your view might it not be appropriate to negotiate? What things do you see as non-negotiable?

For principled negotiation to take place, there needs to be trust on both sides. Trust comes from the belief that both people are entitled to ask for what they want. If you find yourself discussing the merits of what someone is asking for, you are trying to persuade the other that their demands are inappropriate. This is not negotiation. Challenging the other person's value system undermines trust and is likely to lead to an argument. By accepting, not judging, a person's situation, respecting and empathising with their feelings, you create a climate of trust. When pupils realise that you are taking their point of view into account, rather than viewing it with suspicion, they are more likely to meet you half way.

In training

Working in pairs discuss your feelings about the situations below and under what circumstances you would be prepared to negotiate with the child. Be aware of any situations that you feel aren't worth negotiating, or are not negotiable. If you and your partner have different standards, negotiate a way you could comfortably work together.

- A child wants to skip doing your homework this evening.

- A child wants to wear trainers rather than school uniform shoes.

- A talkative child wants to sit next to their friend in your lesson.

- A child wants to do something different from the lesson you have planned.

When you have finished the exercise, negotiate with your partner how to feed back your ideas to the group.

Solutions

When it comes to finding solutions, be creative and enthusiastic, and be prepared to be unconventional. Start from what you have in common, but try not to lose enthusiasm for your own point of view by giving way only to feel bad later. Be clear and specific about what it is you actually want and make sure the other person understands it. If you aren't clear about what is being asked for ask again for clarification or time to think about it. Keep the lines of communication open by asking open-ended questions and inviting the other person's opinion. Check that you have understood, acknowledge their point of view and your own. "I understand that you want to wear trainers, but I cannot agree to your breaking the school rules." Aim for an agreement that both of you have an interest in keeping. Generate as many options as both of you can think of before coming to a conclusion and allow time to think them over. Spend some time considering the consequences of the solutions.

In training
Share how conflicts were solved when you were at school.

The best example I have of a successful negotiation was when I was training as a counsellor. When we were accepted on the course we were told that the first session began at 9.30. By the time the course started, things had changed and lectures were due to start at 9.00. This left me, and several others, in a difficult situation with travel and child care arrangements. We complained to the tutors and they agreed to start lectures at 9.30. However, there were people in the group who, by now, wanted to start at 9.00. At the time I expected the tutors to 'pull rank' and insist on a show of hands, so that one side would have to give way. But they didn't: they waited for us to negotiate. I remember having all sorts of negative thoughts, "This is impossible.....it isn't worth the hassle.....the college is at fault.....the others should give in....." But eventually we came to an agreement that satisfied everyone. The tutors would come at 9.00 and work on a short topic until 9.30. Students who got there early would pass on any relevant information to the latecomers, and the main body of work would begin at 9.30. It was worth spending half an hour or so to negotiate a solution that made sure we all felt comfortable with the arrangements. Any dissatisfaction could have rumbled on all year.

At that time I was more used to the idea of voting than of negotiation. I was tempted to dismiss the others' views as petty or against the rules and use these principles to force some kind of agreement on the group. This view of mine was reinforced by my negative feelings; it seemed impossible to satisfy everyone. However, I realised that when minority feelings are marginalised or ignored, dissatisfaction does not go away. When people feel as though their needs are unimportant this influences their relationship to the group. These feelings have a habit of surfacing every time the group needs to co-operate. For example, I know of a school where a majority decision to change the times of the school day left some parents feeling so angry and resentful that they felt unable to co-operate willingly on any further joint projects. These feelings lasted for several years. It can be seen that negotiation skills are useful in interpersonal communications and as a way of increasing equality of opportunity in group situations.

When the Religious Society of Friends (Quakers) have meetings to make plans for the future of their group or Meeting as it is known, decisions are reached only when all the people present agree. Votes are never taken and everyone's view is treated with respect. The Clerk of the Meeting keeps rewriting the proposal, assessing the feeling of the meeting, until it is agreed by everyone.

In training
As a group, share your experiences of situations where minority views have not been taken into account. If you were in the minority, how did you feel? Or how did you feel being in the majority? What effect did these feelings have?

Giving Feedback

Teachers have many occasions for giving feedback; writing reports, record-keeping, assessing performance and verbal comments on behaviour and work. Giving feedback means giving information to someone about their behaviour which they may use to affect their subsequent behaviour.

> In training
> As a group, think of situations where you might want to give feedback. What are the advantages of giving feedback? What are the risks involved?

When you comment on children's behaviour and performance they are given the opportunity to learn more about themselves and the effect they have on others. Giving feedback shows warmth because the children are aware that you are interested in them and notice what they do. It is also a way of being genuine. When your pupils know that you express your thoughts and feelings about their behaviour and work, they know where they stand. Because feedback is non-judgmental, children are encouraged to develop their potential and become aware of their personal standards without being defensive because they feel criticised.

I have noticed that children who come to the centre where I work seem surprised, even touched, when we give them feedback about themselves. It seems that they are not used to being noticed without judgement. Children's behaviour is praised or criticised but not necessarily constructively mirrored back to them. "You looked apprehensive when it was your turn to give your talk, but by the end you seemed much more relaxed. Is that right?"

Feedback is non-judgmental
The important thing to remember about feedback is that it is non-judgmental and value-free. In other words you describe what you see and experience, rather than evaluate the situation. For example, "When Jane got upset, you laughed," rather than, "You are an unsympathetic person for laughing," or, "You answered that question

really quickly and gave us a lot of interesting information," rather than, "Well done!" Your tone of voice is important too, because a statement can sound like a criticism even if it is a factual description of the situation.

Be specific

Feedback is of little value unless it is clear and useful, so when giving any kind of feedback, make it specific. It is more satisfying to hear, "I like the colours in your picture.....your tidy desk.....the way your hair is cut at the back," rather than the general comment such as "I like your picture.....your tidiness.....your hair." It is particularly important to be specific when writing reports. Descriptive examples of behaviour or work convey constructive information that can be acted upon, and are less likely to be experienced as critical or patronising. For example, "James spent 20 minutes out of a 40 minute lesson talking to his friend," is more useful than "James is a talkative child," or "Jane's handwriting is neat and she sets her work out attractively and clearly," rather than, "Jane's written work is good."

Own the feedback

When giving feedback it is important to speak for yourself by using words like 'I', 'me', 'my' or 'mine'. The use of these words shows that you are expressing your own thoughts and perceptions, and owning them as yours and not claiming them to be a universal truth. As a rule, people feel safer talking about their perceptions in a way that separates the person from the statement as in,"It is difficult to work with you," rather than, "I am having difficulty working with you." If you listen to an interview on television, people who are talking about themselves, more often than not, use the word 'you' instead of 'I'. Perhaps this is because we have been brought up to believe that making statements about ourselves is a sign of arrogance. We often avoid direct self-disclosure because of the risk of criticism. However, this way of talking is confusing; we can lose track of who the 'you' refers to. It can also be irritating when we don't hold the same opinion as the speaker as in, for example, "Well, you do feel stupid when you don't know the answer." Statements like these assume that everyone feels the same. People talking in a group often fall into the habit of speaking on behalf of the group, without checking the accuracy of their perceptions. Distancing ourselves like this also reinforces the notion that standards are universal, and attempts to make things 'safer' for the speaker.

If you give feedback without taking responsibility for it, and give the recipient the idea that you are speaking on behalf of others or a set of universal standards, your feedback is more likely to be experienced as a put-down.

In training
As a group, change these statements so that the speaker takes responsibility for them.

  This has gone on for long enough!
  When you are alone you feel rejected.
  We don't behave like that here.
  One can't do everything.
  It is too cold in here.
  Rap is rubbish.

Then try to ensure you own all your statements and opinions in your training group.

Acknowledge your feelings

When giving feedback about a situation, expressing the way you feel about it gives a clear indication of the effect it is having on you. However, it isn't always appropriate to act out your feelings. They can be acknowledged verbally without leaving others to cope with the actuality of them. For example during a child's talk about their pet in an English lesson, "I feel frightened when you bring your mouse too close to me. Please don't do it," is more appropriate than rushing terrified from the room clutching the bottoms of your trousers!

Feelings are not always apparent to others because most people have been taught to hide them. Also, without realising it, we can give mixed messages when we don't want to show our feelings, like smiling when we are angry or upset. When feelings are unacknowledged, others are aware that something is going on and fill the gap by imagining or guessing what it might be. Or they respond to the smile or the tone of voice, rather than the content of the words.

When acknowledging the way you feel it is crucial to own the feelings as your own. People develop a range of ways of disowning their feelings. They may distance themselves from their feelings by talking about them in an abstract way, as in "There is some concern," instead of admitting they are worried about something. We are all tempted to say, "I'm fine," when we are anything but fine. We often fall into the trap of blaming others for the way we feel, "You make me angry!" rather than, "I feel angry." Although other people do have an effect on the way we feel, blaming them for causing the feeling is a way of avoiding responsibility for our feelings and their consequences. Someone else in the same situation could feel entirely differently, so no-one directly *causes* another's feelings.

In training
In pairs, identify the ways you express feelings. Which feeling do you have difficulty expressing? Which can you express easily? Think of some situations where someone has blamed you for their feelings. Share how that felt with the group.

Being aware of my own feelings and communicating them, where appropriate, to pupils has also been useful for me. I have found that when I can remember to tell children the way I feel about their behaviour has sometimes brought about a sympathetic response when I didn't expect it. When I told a child that I felt frustrated when he talked whilst I was trying to explain something, he looked sheepish and stopped. By telling him how I felt, rather then just telling him to stop talking and listen, I had more of an effect.

Suggest an alternative

When you have given feedback about what you have seen happening in a situation, it is often useful to suggest an alternative. This gives the child a way of putting things right and means that the final outcome of the interaction results in a positive feeling rather than a negative one. Be clear and specific about the kind of change you want and consider the effects this change will have. For example, "When you rush into the classroom noisily, I feel startled. I'd like you to come in quietly and wait for a while before talking to me."

Invite a response

After you have given your feedback it is important to invite a response or ask for some help from the recipient. This conveys respect to the child because you trust them to want to be helpful. It also reduces the possibility of your observation being seen as a put-down or an attack. The recipient then has an opportunity to give their point of view. By giving them the opportunity for self-criticism and explanation the child will be more open to further suggestions. "This piece of work seems much improved. What do you think?" I'm sure we have all had the experience of being criticised for something which we had a perfectly good reason for doing. When people decide our motives without checking it can be extremely frustrating.

Using feedback as a challenge to unacceptable behaviour

Because people use criticism to put others down, any attempt to challenge unacceptable behaviour can be perceived as negative. Consequently the recipient can feel bad about themselves and become hurt or angry; this fact often deters us from challenging the behaviour. However, when unacceptable behaviour is ignored the unpleasant feelings that accompany it do not go away. Either we carry the discomfort around with us or matters come to a head in the form of an argument - often about something else unconnected to the original situation. If you follow the guidelines for giving feedback, it is possible to reflect back unacceptable behaviour and reduce the potential for misunderstanding and conflict. The main thing to remember about feedback, is that when you give it, it is a way of showing that you care, and an opportunity for change. "I am trying to explain something to you, and you are looking out of the window. I'm feeling irritated every time I look at you. What do we need to do so that you can join in the lesson?"

In training
In pairs, think of the times as a child and adult when you were unfairly criticised. How did it feel? How could it have been handled better? Feedback to the group.

When giving feedback on unacceptable behaviour, take some time to identify your intention in giving it and whether it is in everyone's interest. Consider whether it is the right time or place for the feedback to be accepted; (the middle of the dinner queue may not be appropriate!) If possible, it is better to start with something positive, then describe what you see as the problem. "Last lesson you were really helpful to other children, but today I have seen you shouting angrily at someone three or four times. I feel concerned. What is going on?"

When challenging unacceptable behaviour, always state what you want changed in a clear way. So often we moan or complain without giving the child a way of putting things right. "I find your views interesting, but cannot always read your handwriting. I would like you to practise using larger letters." This is more helpful than, "Your work is always untidy and impossible to read."

In training

As a group, use the guidelines below to devise some constructive feedback for the following situations. A child grins at his friends when another child is upset. A child gives in untidy work. A colleague is always borrowing things and not returning them. A colleague's class makes a noise that interferes with your lessons.

Guidelines for giving feedback:
  Start with something positive.
  Describe what you see.
  Explain how you think/feel. (What effect is the behaviour having on you?)
  Suggest an alternative if you have one.
  Invite their opinion with open-ended questions. (How do you feel? What do you think?)....

Of course, if you are used to giving feedback and challenging unacceptable behaviour in different ways from those described here, you cannot change your style overnight. Communication is a spontaneous activity, you soon dry up if you have to think too much before you speak. However, set yourself some small targets that are easily achieved.

Receiving feedback

In your professional life there are times when you will be the recipient of feedback. You can ask for it after interviews and will be given it during teacher appraisal. From time to time, you may get feedback from colleagues, parents and children. You may even wish to ask others for feedback. Listening to feedback is a way of finding out your strengths and weakness, and of building up a picture of yourself, by comparing the views of others with those of your own. If you can handle getting feedback abut yourself, you give the children a good role model of an adult who is comfortable with themselves. Although it is not customary to allow people to discuss our shortcomings with us, the more usual way we have of avoiding feedback means that we leave things until they get to boiling point and blow up into an argument. Either that or we put ourselves in the position of being unaware of a situation that everyone else is moaning about.

If you can learn to accept feedback gracefully, you get a better idea of what is working well and a chance to put right the things that can be improved upon. The most important thing to remember is that no-one is perfect and that all behaviour is appropriate sometimes! Be on your own side and take responsibility for your behaviour. If you are late, irritable, can't speak out at meetings, or get angry easily, these behaviours are easier both for yourself and others to live with if you can acknowledge them, respect that you have good reasons for feeling the way you do and not blame anyone else for making you shy, angry, late or irritable. Everyone has strengths and weaknesses, good days and bad ones; and even when we don't do things that meet up with our highest standards it is good to remember that we are doing the best we can at that time.

It actually isn't the weaknesses, that creates the problems, but being so touchy or sensitive about them, that other people have to pretend they are not there. This means that you cannot make plans which openly take them into account. For example, I once worked with someone who was good company and was able to make good relationships with the children. For some reason he didn't feel safe enough to accept the fact that he disliked administration. I hated having to order stock or arrange outings with him because I could never rely on him to book the coach or bring the right catalogues. But if I reminded him or asked him if he had done the things he had agreed to do, he would get irritable and complain that I was checking up on him or fussing. If he could have admitted his shortcomings, we could have worked things out together and allocated the work according to our strengths.

To accept feedback gracefully, resist the temptation to instantly defend yourself. Take time to listen to the feedback and check out that you have understood it by reflective listening. You might need to ask for some further clarification. When you have understood it, you may feel it appropriate to ask the other person what they want you to do about it. Again resist the temptation to beat your breast and offer all sorts of atonement or give some criticism back to even up the score! Calmly evaluate what has been said, ask for time to think, if you need it, and check whether others have the same feelings about your behaviour. The feedback might only be one person's perception of you. Or maybe the feedback says more about the giver than you. When you have understood the feedback, decide what you want to do as a result of it.

When you are able to discuss your limitations, other people, more often than not respect your courage, and find you easier to work with than people who are touchy or easily upset by feedback.

At the centre where I work, we give the young people opportunities to give the staff feedback. They are well aware of the rules, that it isn't an opportunity to be rude or destructive, especially as they have their own turn in the 'hot seat'. I am always surprised by the things they notice and appreciate. I am often told by the young people that I am too fussy and expect too much of them. I have thought about this feedback and checked it out with my colleagues and decided to tone down some of my expectations. However, I also realised that I will keep some of my high expectations because I do not believe in having second class aspirations for pupils.

In training
Make a list of you shortcomings (don't go mad!).
Which ones are you comfortable with, and which do
you wish you didn't have? If it's appropriate share
lists with rest of the group. Do you agree with others'
lists? How does it feel to share your list? Share
feelings to the group.

Feedback can also be given in the form of compliments. Sometimes
these can be just as hard to take as criticisms. When someone pays
you a compliment, either about you or something you've done,
resist the temptation to reduce the size of the praise or even refuse
to accept it. "Your room looks nice; you've worked hard on it."
"Oh, it doesn't, it's a mess really. It took not time at all." Rebuffing
compliments can be hurtful for the giver as well as a way of putting
yourself down.

In training
Give a genuine compliment to someone who has been
primed to rebuff it. Feed back how it felt not to have
your compliment welcomed or well received.
Give each other a general compliment, practise
thanking the giver for their observation, resisting the
temptation to 'bat it off' or qualify it in any way.

Praise
It is very easy to take positive attributes for granted, and only notice
when things go wrong. Although teachers are generally aware of
the importance of praise, as a culture we seem to be embarrassed or
suspicious of both giving and receiving compliments. We worry it
will make the recipient conceited or that if we accept compliments

we will be seen as conceited. Many adults seem to think that criticism spurs a child on to make greater efforts. It seems to me, however, that criticism undermines confidence even if it does challenge people into action. It also seems that when someone notices your good points it can both spur you on to greater efforts and make you feel good whenever you remember it. Because of our self-deprecatory culture we seem better at putting ourselves down than acknowledging our strengths. Yet, if we cannot feel good about ourselves, it is hard to feel genuinely good about others.

When giving praise, the guidelines for giving feedback are useful. If our praise is evaluative it can, in the long run, be as unhelpful as blame or criticism. Being told who you are, even if it is complimentary can be an uncomfortable experience. What happens if you do not feel able to live up to the praise, or do not really value the qualities you are being praised for? Praise can be used as a way of controlling behaviour and limiting self-expression. If, for example, children are praised for being quiet and submissive, the implication is that noisy and assertive behaviour is disapproved of. Evaluative praise, used as a reward also encourages a dependence on external approval. Ideally, we need to be our own judge of our self-worth and standards.

In training
Working in pairs remember the times when someone has given you some praise. What kind of praise feels good and bad?

There is an important difference between praising with "You are....." statements and giving praise by following the guidelines for giving feedback. By owning the praise and being descriptive rather than evaluative, praise becomes more satisfying and constructive. For example, "I like the way the sink looks nice and clean, after all that work you put in," or, "I enjoyed reading that article; it gave me much to think about." Rather than, "You're a clean person," or "You're a goo writer."

Self-assessment

We surely know ourselves better than anyone else knows us, yet many people find it difficult to assess their own strengths accurately. We tend to feel it is safer to leave assessment to others because they are somehow more able to recognise our capabilities. But in a competitive world, where giving compliments seems to go against the grain, it is possible to go through most of our working life feeling unrecognised. If we want our children to grow up with confidence and to develop feelings of self-worth we need to help them to know themselves and be the ultimate judge of their own character. This means giving them the opportunity to assess themselves and to be aware of any assessments that are made about them and be involved in the making of them. It also means developing our own ability to assess ourselves.

In training
Working in pairs identify some of your strengths. Feedback to the group what it felt like to tell someone of your good points.

When I was working in a prison, I used to keep a record of my pupils' marks with a comment about their future needs in a book that I kept on my desk. Once, I left the room for a while; when I came back most of the boys were crowded round the book and discussing what was in it. At first, we all felt as though they had been doing something they shouldn't! Then some of them began to argue, "I should have had a better mark than that....I don't need to improve my handwriting." My concerns about whether they had invaded my privacy or not seemed unimportant compared to the way they seemed to care! Somewhere buried inside, these supposedly hardened criminals, was the idea that what was written in my book mattered! I let each one of them re-do the work in question to get a better mark, I also agreed to negotiate any further comment to be written in my book. That afternoon taught me a lot. They had a clear idea of their own performance and wanted to challenge mine when the two didn't match. I have always left my record book on my desk ever since.

Summaries
Conflict Management
Spotting differences 5 causes:

Values	the difference between what I think is important and what you think is important
Understanding	the difference between what I understand and what you understand
Style	the difference between the way I do something and the way you do it
Opinions	the difference between what you think and what I think
Interests	the difference between what I want and what you want

Teaching Styles
Aggressive - win/lose
This style uses put-downs, shouting, sulking, threatening, challenging, sarcasm, banging doors, pointing fingers, getting own way but leaving the other person feeling bad.

Passive - lose/lose.
Passive people do nothing, hope it will work out, go behind people's backs, have little eye contact, explain, apologise, retreat.

Assertive - win/win
Assertive people are generally calm, relaxed, have direct eye contact, are confident, respect others' feelings, empathise, listen, explore options, negotiate, look for resolution, check out responses.

Assertiveness Techniques
Be positive - about yourself and others.
Know your rights - be clear about what you want and your right to want it.

Express feelings, opinions and wishes calmly and openly.
Be comfortable with your own strengths and weaknesses.

Fogging
Agree with words but don't accept any blame.
Accept the truth but don't accept the blame.
Ask for more information.

Broken record
Be persistent with requests.
Empathise and be persistent.

Negotiation
Identify the differences between you.
Put yourself in the other's shoes. (Convey your understanding with reflective listening and ask for clarification if necessary).
Don't blame someone for asking.
Don't argue the merits of one view over another.
Listen actively.
Is this issue non-negotiable or not important enough to you?
Is this the right time and place to negotiate?
Am I in the right frame of mind?
Be specific about what you want. (Stick to the point; avoid red-herrings).
Ask for 100% of what you want. (Don't ask for less because you feel guilty or more so that your compromise will not be genuine.
Obtain opinions.
Look for a win/win outcome, offer compromise, establish what you have in common.
Believe that it will work.
Allow enough time.
Be creative with solutions.
Allow enough time to consider options.

Feedback

Giving Feedback

Feedback should always be non-judgmental

Describe what you see without bias

Be specific

Own the feedback

Acknowledge your feelings about the issue in question

Take care to use a warm, not critical, tone of voice

Suggest alternative responses

Invite responses

Using feedback to challenge unacceptable behaviour

Follow guidelines for giving feedback

Be sure of your motivation for giving this feedback

Be clear about what you want changing

Keep your feelings about the behaviour separate from
the person

Receiving feedback

Resist the temptation to feel criticised or blamed

Resist temptation to rebuff compliments

Encourage feedback

Check that you have understood the feedback, don't jump to
conclusions

Acknowledge your shortcomings and don't 'beat yourself
up' about them

Acknowledge your strengths

Creating a Supportive Atmosphere

5

In the classroom

Most teachers are very aware of the importance of the 'feel' of a classroom. They arrange pictures and work on the walls, bring in plants and interesting objects, and try to ensure that the colours and furnishings are as comfortable and welcoming as finance and practicality will allow. Such attention to detail, in addition to providing a stimulating environment, makes children feel welcome and important.

However, the way teachers relate to their pupils is more of an influence on the atmosphere within the classroom than the physical surroundings. If you want to provide person-centred core conditions, you need more than just the skills to communicate them. You need also to be clear about the kind of teacher you are because different teaching styles encourage the development of different qualities. It is possible, for example, to use assertiveness techniques as a way of controlling children rather than empowering them. It is important to identify, explore and question your beliefs about the way children should be treated to find out whether they correspond to your objectives.

As well as the *physical* environment in a classroom each teacher creates a *psychological* one with their teaching style. Their teaching style is expressed by the way they communicate with children. It is also conveyed through their standards and the way the 'dos and don'ts' of the classroom are chosen and upheld. These processes, and the values implicit in them, give the children constant feedback regarding their self-worth.

But how do we choose our teaching style and standards? And what kind of effect do these have on young people? We do not often have the opportunity to examine this aspect of teaching. Training courses look at children's development, materials, curricula, teaching theories but rarely at the individual teachers themselves. Yet *the way teachers teach and behave is of crucial significance in the classroom*, and affects both academic and social learning.

Standards.
The words 'decline in standards' are often used to express a general dissatisfaction with the performance of young people today. They imply that parents and teachers are failing to pass on a consensus of values to the next generation. But in my experience, no-one is deliberately trying to undermine standards. They are either unclear as to what standards they are supposed to be upholding or unsure of how to pass on such an abstract concept as standards.

It used to be simple; "Children should be seen and not heard" was enough of a guide for everyone to know what was expected of them, that is, obedience and conformity. These days there are far more expectations of a teacher than simply keeping children in line. Victorian values are no longer a sufficient guide, we need some new guidelines that acknowledge the realities of the twentieth-century life. Yet all we seem to have are the rather vague expectations of others, and a readiness of some sections of society to blame and criticise when things appear to be unsatisfactory, or when things are changing faster than they can keep up with.

In training
As a group, brainstorm the kind of pupil society expects teachers to produce and the kind of teacher society expects you to be.
In pairs, identify the way you feel about, and respond to, the following:

noise	untidiness	low marks
boisterousness	jokes	arguments
curiosity	awkward questions	

How much does the opinion of others influence your reaction? Feedback to the group.

Standards can be a way of giving ourselves and the children a hard time. Without consciously developed personal standards, people tend to try to live up to the abstract, and often impractical and outdated ideals of others. Also because we feel obliged to live up to the expectations of others, our own standards seem to be of secondary importance.

Children are expected to be neat and tidy, but not too neat and tidy, because then they become obsessive; polite and obedient, but having a mind of their own when initiative is required. Rows of fresh-faced school children singing hymns in assembly, or busily engaged in the classroom are what is 'required'. People jump to conclusions too; if they see a child behaving angrily, looking untidy or doing nothing. They make instant assumptions about what is happening, based more often than not on the worst possible interpretation. If we constantly expect ourselves to cater to expectations like these, we are doomed to failure.

Firstly, these kinds of standards assume that there is only one way to be 'good'. Secondly, they take no account of the fact that growing children need to learn by making mistakes, acting out their personality, and experimenting with different ideas and behaviours. Qualities such as creativity, individuality, exploration and initiative, without which human beings could not survive, seem to be valued only as a finished product. People seem unable to tolerate the necessary learning stages in between. This is also true in schools which tend to value most highly the 'conforming academic.'

In training

Make a list of what standards in the classroom are important to you. Rate them in order of importance. Discuss these with someone else. Feed back to the group any feelings you had about different standards, or the same standards. Are any of these standards not yours? Discuss how you can be appropriately genuine with a) children, b) parents and c) colleagues.

When we try to live up to the expectations of others, it is easy to feel that our pupils' behaviour and performance is a reflection on our skill. Teachers feel blamed and judged when pupils' behaviour seems below standard. So we become anxious for our pupils to be seen as 'good' by others, and this passes on to the next generation the belief in the importance of other people's expectations.

When I started working at the Youth Justice Centre, I had to learn that although we could control the young people and compel them to behave in an acceptable manner, it did not solve any of their problems. They would continue expressing them somewhere else; on the streets, at home, or when they returned to main-stream school. However, by observing their unacceptable behaviour, we could identify the way they got into trouble and work with it by mirroring it back to them. The children expected us to control them and in the beginning would blame us when they got into trouble. "You should have stopped us!" We had to teach them to be responsible for their own actions and to take the consequences. If, for example, a child swore a lot, he would be given feedback such as, "We don't want you to come out with us, because you will show us up!" - not just from the adults but from the whole group. This kind of feedback is more effective than banning swearing. When children experience the consequences of their actions in this way it has a permanent effect on their behaviour.

Congruence
We all have different tolerance levels and these change from day to day, depending on our health, strength and circumstances. The myth that we are supposed to be consistent is one that many of us try to live up to. We need to recognise the effects of our behaviour, and take responsibility for our levels of tolerance and communicate this fact to the children. If we can say, "I've not got much patience today, so if you want to do anything complicated you will have to sort it out for yourselves," we show the children that we are human and comfortable with our imperfections. We also give them clear guidelines as to what to expect from us and what is required from them. When, for example, we struggle to be patient all the time, we will fail. Trying to be constantly patient, wise, caring, etc. is stressful. We cannot keep it up everyday and end up feeling exhausted or venting our frustration on the children or our families, because they expect us to be patient all the time. It is not impatience or irritability that causes confusion for children, but incongruence - acting in a patient way when we feel the opposite is easily spotted, and gives confusing, mixed messages to children.

Growing up is a messy business, children need to express their feelings, their doubts about the system, their individuality and to make mistakes. If they are met by adults who can handle their needs with respect and warmth, they will be more likely to develop emotional maturity. Teachers who allow their children this kind of constructive freedom need to be courageous and sure of themselves. It makes things easier if you are quite clear about what you are doing and operating from a definite, thought-out set of standards.

What kind of leader am I?

As well as identifying our own standards, or the things that are important to us, we also need to give some conscious thought to the style of teaching we want to adopt. To some extent this decision will be informed by our personality but there is also a large space for choice in this. I have found it useful to remind myself at regular intervals that 'I reap what I sow,' in other words, the way I am will affect, both positively and negatively, the behaviour of all those I come into contact with. If you are just at the teacher training stage this will be the ideal opportunity to form your style, but even if you have been teaching for some time you may feel the style you have isn't working or maybe you are just ready for a change.

Basically there are three teaching styles: authoritarian, permissive and assertive (which could also be called person-centred). Most teachers instinctively use a mixture of styles depending the occasion, their mood or that of the children. The types outlined below do not describe actual teachers but an abstract example of each style. They are hypothetical and expressed here in a fairly extreme way to make the point; however they are useful guides to use when trying to identify your standards, expectations and objectives.

The *authoritarian* teacher feels that, being a trained professional, they know what is best for their pupils and should impress on them the behaviour, thoughts and feelings that are considered correct. They are the boss and ultimate judge of right and wrong behaviour, and believe that their values represent those of society at large. Authoritarian teachers do not attempt to involve their pupils in identifying common goals or negotiating boundaries and ground rules, but feel obliged to have total control over such processes. When children deviate from their rules, they are perceived as a threat to their authority. Because their standards are fixed, they can be critical of any differences of belief, values, styles and opinions. Consequently, authoritarian teachers are controlling of conflict. They know exactly what kind of information they wish to impart and stick rigidly to their plans showing little flexibility in accommodating their pupils' differing needs or giving little space for their contributions. It can be difficult for teachers who have a different teaching style to relate to children who are influenced by an authoritarian teacher. This is because of the perception that anyone less authoritarian is weak and somehow lacking. Authoritarian teachers do not show personal feelings and tend to be most comfortable when they have a professional relationship with children, parents and colleagues. Consequently, they do not mix with the children at break times or in a social way during outings and activities. They are predictable; children know what is expected of them and this provides a measure of security for them. Although authoritarian teachers care about the children, pupils have to compete for their approval because it is conditional on behaviour. Often, they command respect because our society is authoritarian by tradition. The only responses possible to the authoritarian style are fight, flight or submission. When the popular press calls for more discipline in schools, the implication is that teachers are no longer authoritarian enough and that is why children do not behave properly.

Permissive teachers, are either unclear about boundaries and how to put them into effect or do not feel that they have the right to influence children's behaviour. They may well have the same objectives as an assertive teacher, but either believe or hope that the children will achieve these goals naturally. Consequently they neither think out their boundaries and ground rules nor communicate them to their pupils. When things go wrong or issues arise, permissive teachers may feel responsible for putting everything right, react with anger and frustration, or leave the children to sort things out for themselves. Conflict is ignored or 'buried'. Permissive teachers can be distracted from their objectives because their attention tends to go to the highest bidder, the nosiest or the most persistent. Although they are predictably permissive, their reactions to situations are unpredictable because they are influenced by others. This means that they cannot be relied upon to stick to the point, to give their undivided attention or to sort out disputes fairly. Children tend to consider permissive teachers weak and unfair. They respond to them by constantly pushing in order to reach some predictable, secure boundaries. Permissive teachers can be experienced as nurturing because they allow children to grow without too much adult interference and give of themselves without expecting anything in return. In the 60s, there were many experiments with the permissive style of teaching, in an attempt to develop an alternative to the authoritarian style. Most teachers soon realised that giving children, rather than the teacher, the power, was not a practical alternative to the authoritarian style. Although the permissive style encouraged the development of more child-centred teaching methods which involved the children in their own learning, in my experience, the whole package was rarely implemented for long. Yet the permissive teaching style is still being blamed for the supposed decline of standards in schools.

The *assertive* teacher values the children and respects both their own needs and those of their pupils. Power and control are not on the agenda. Responsibility is shared and the aim is for the development of co-operation, negotiation, self-discipline and trust. A common purpose is identified and boundaries and ground rules are worked out together. Conflict is resolved and used creatively where possible. Assertive teachers are predictable and acknowledge feelings by allowing both themselves and the children to be human. They use feedback to mirror behaviour and can say "No," with firmness and without blame. Assertive teaching has grown out of developments in person-centred teaching and interpersonal skills training. Children take time to learn to trust, and respond to an assertive teacher, because more often than not they are used to other styles of teaching and parenting. To become an assertive teacher requires a commitment to training and personal development and a belief in the intrinsic equal value of all individuals.

In training
Working in pairs.
1. Remember your own teachers. How did you feel abut them and their different teaching styles? Contd......What were the things you liked/disliked about them? 2. What is your own teaching style? Are you happy with it? Feedback to the group. 3. Brainstorm the advantage and disadvantages of all three styles.

Self-esteem

Whilst all three styles are appropriate sometimes, it can be seen that the predominance of one style of leadership over another produces varying effects on a child's self-esteem or image of themselves.

There are many things that influence a child's self-perception. School is a significant one because it is the main arena for a child's contact with the world outside their home. In school, children learn how to interact with their peers and adults from different families and different cultures. They become aware of their differences and similarities to others. They also build up a sense of how far the way they feel about themselves matches up to the 'ideal person', an image that is implied by the qualities which are valued, admired, rewarded and imitated in school. Their teachers' styles of teaching and choice of standards influences whether a child comes to feel accepted for who he or she is. This in turn affects the child's self-esteem and ability to accept and feel positive about themselves; and ultimately how they form relationships with others and how they learn.

We all have needs, but I hesitate to generalise about the needs of others, so I will speak of my own needs; you can decide if what I say matches your experience too. I need attention and to feel a sense of belonging. I need to feel I have control over my lives and that I have security. I need to feel useful and free to explore and express my independence. And ultimately, I need to feel liked and likeable, that my friends enjoy my company and find me interesting. The way our needs are responded to can either encourage the development of the kind of self-esteem that leads to personal integrity or to anxiety and negativity. And current thinking by some neurologists even suggests that mental illnesses such as depression and schizophrenia have social triggers.

> In training
> What are the effects of high and low self-esteem, and how do they affect you?

Positive Messages
If we give children negative messages about their performance and behaviour when expressing their needs, they begin to feel negative about themselves and unacceptable and vulnerable when they have needs. Negative messages undermine their confidence in their ability to think, act, learn, and express individuality.

In the sections dealing with introjected values and the effects of put-downs we examined the ways in which we acquire and communicate negative thoughts about ourselves and others. The negative thoughts and feelings you have about yourself generally come from the messages you received about yourself when you were young. When working with children it is important that you try to avoid the build up of further unhelpful introjected values in their minds and give them positive, useful and affirming messages about themselves.

> In training
> Remember the positive and negative things said to you when you were at school. Did these have any lasting effects? Share with the group if appropriate.

We seem, as a culture, to use negative energy more than positive energy to achieve our goals. If you think about it, you are more likely to be asked to attend a staff meeting because you ought to, rather than be asked to go because your contribution is valued or enjoyed. Yet, I find it far easier to get the energy to do something when I am invited with a positive reason rather than a negative one. When I am asked to something because otherwise the person will be angry, upset or regard me as being lazy, selfish or of failing in my duty, if I act on the request, I do it out of guilt. If I refuse the request I feel rebellious.

In order to facilitate self-esteem we need to create a climate where people feel they are accepted, they matter and that they are capable of coping, by giving positive affirming messages whenever possible. Positive thinking is empowering and develops self-esteem. We have looked at the way we can be positive whilst giving feedback and challenging unacceptable behaviour where we mirror back a child's behaviour rather than evaluate it. Being positive also extends to giving instructions, making requests and giving encouragement.

Boundaries & ground rules

There have to be dos and don'ts in every classroom. These need to be clear. If children have been involved in discussing these boundaries they will be more likely to keep them because they will be finding their own rules rather than just agreeing with someone else's. It is worth spending time with every class telling them what your boundaries are, asking their opinion of them, explaining how you feel and why you need them and giving them the opportunity to identify their own boundaries. When you have identified a set of boundaries it is useful to make a note of them and decide what will happen when they are crossed. It may also be useful to revise them from time to time especially if they do not seem to be working. It is much easier to have an orderly classroom when everyone has responsibility for keeping it that way.

It is also important to be positive when working on boundaries. It is more effective and affirming for a child if you say what you do want rather than what you don't want to happen; "I'd like you to keep the classroom tidy." This means that the child is doing something you have asked for rather than avoiding doing something that would displease you. In the same way, if you can say something like, "I'd like you to clean your shoes," rather than, "You look untidy," you are using positive rather than negative energy to achieve results. Framing boundaries in this way is more effective.

If boundaries are what you don't do then ground rules are what you do do. Again it is more effective to involve the children in identifying ground rules and being positive. For example, "In our classroom we respect other people's differences and abilities." By spending time with the children discussing the way they feel about being in the classroom, the behaviour of others, you can encourage them to be respectful and supportive of each other.

Hopes & concerns
There is another area worth exploring with children. By giving them the opportunity to express what they want from school they experience their wishes being catered for, are involved in making choices and become aware of their responsibilities in the process. If you also give children a chance to express their worries, you open up an area where these issues can be dealt with, rather than leaving the children to cope with them by themselves. They may, for example, be worried about getting behind when they don't understand something or they may be concerned about a group of noisy children who they fear will disrupt lessons or that they may be bullied at break-times.

Discussions like the ones outlined above teach children to acknowledge and respect their own perceptions. Acting on the information received from the pupils gives them the experience of an adult who respects their wishes and feelings that helps them to feel secure and valued. This is not so much an exercise for choosing what to study, that is already defined by the National Curriculum, it is a way of bringing objectives into the open, making contracts about how these objectives can be achieved, discussing approaches and giving the children an opportunity to express their wishes and their fears.

Encouragement

Reminding a child of a time when they tried hard and succeeded is more likely to encourage them to keep on trying than any amount of telling them what will happen if they don't work hard.

If we express the belief that a child cannot sit next to a friend without talking or carrying a jug of water without spilling it we are telling them that they are untrustworthy or incapable. If we ask children to do things from a negative standpoint we remind them that they can fail. It is much more inspiring to do something because it produces pleasure, than to do it to avoid censure. If you tell children what you want, what you like, they can do something to please you rather than not do something to avoid displeasing you.

****

If you think about it, adults can generally choose where they spend their time. If they join a club or find themselves in a job where their self-esteem takes a battering, they can try to change things or leave. When children experience school as a place where they are blamed for their problems, rejected as individuals or perceived as failures what can they do about it? They rarely have any control over their environment, their only course of action is to truant, misbehave or withdraw. Yet school is a place where they are obliged to spend about a quarter of their time, in their most formative years.

The creation of the core conditions and the skills which can be used to convey warmth, genuineness and empathy create a 'child-centred' atmosphere which encourages self discovery and the growth of self-respect and trust. A classroom becomes a place where children feel cared for and safe to experiment with their behaviour and learning. School becomes an environment where children can experience positive relationships, show initiative and express autonomy, qualities which are much needed for the future of our society.

In the staffroom

When I started work at my first school, it never occurred to me to ask the staff about the kind of support available if problems arose. I assumed it was all down to me. I took on my class of 43 in an Educational Priority school, as they were then called, and I set about surviving without expecting much help from anyone else. I was lucky, the school was old-fashioned enough to have a system of mothering probationary teachers. But mothering has its drawbacks; I tended to have to pay for it by being submissive at staff meetings. And although I could send pupils to the head if they got too much for me, she'd send them right back again if she was busy! I never felt *entitled* to support. There was no specific time for me to talk about my work and no-one designated to support or manage me. Asking for help was a risky business, I was worried that if I asked for help too often it would look as though I couldn't cope and I wasn't sure how much was too often. I was aware, too, that everyone was busy and I felt guilty when other teachers spent time helping me. Yet I would go home unable to relax; feeling concerned about particular children, unsure how to deal with them, stressed after arguments and apprehensive about the following day. I would talk about work until my flatmates were sick of the subject. The only people I could really talk to were other young teachers, which was useful but still a case of the blind leading the blind! I would have loved someone to talk to who was experienced and could give advice without judging me and finding me wanting because I needed help; someone who wasn't doing me a favour.

When expensively trained teachers give up teaching because they can't cope, it can be just because they lacked support, not because they are poor teachers. There is great value in groups of teachers talking things over with each other, especially as a staff team in a person-centred climate using the core conditions. Teachers need time allocated to be able to put together their own support network, one that suits their school and circumstances. Time to talk about issues that concern them and, if necessary, support from outside, to help them find ways to move forward.

In training
Split the group into threes or fours and brainstorm the following:
• the times when you have needed support,
• the kind of support you would like and
• how this support could be made available.

Organising support

If there isn't already a support system in your school (and if there is you may want to change it) you can put it on the agenda and suggest it as something that can be explored on in-service training days, ideally with the help of an outside facilitator initially. It is important that any discussions of this nature are carried out in a climate of the core conditions. It does not seem to be generally recognised in the teaching profession that you have a right to support if you need it and that asking for it isn't a sign of failure.

When you have established that a support network would be beneficial, you can spend time identifying the ways you can actually support each other. This can take the form of simply sharing experience, ideas and tips, listening and supporting each other when you've had a stressful experience, identifying situations that cause conflict and ways of changing them and developing strategies for supporting each other when problems arise in the classroom. This process takes time, especially in the beginning, but without it it's like sending a passenger liner to sea without any lifeboats.

In training
Individually. Think about the problems you have with individual children. Do the same for particular classes. Does the school system, such as expectations about uniform and homework, create problems? What kind of support would help you deal with these problems?

Parents

My job often entails working with the parents who don't come willingly to school. However, I have never met a parent yet who wasn't interested in their child's education. I have met parents who have felt alienated by the educational system. Many parents need support because they feel unable to respond to the demands of school even if they agree with the principles. They are unwilling to face yet another interview with the Head to be told that their child is behaving badly, because they feel powerless to improve things and blamed for being inadequate parents. They often feel their opinions are without value when faced with the experts. This process can lead them, whether consciously or unconsciously, to reject what the schools stands for and opt out of responsibility. Complaints from school can cause considerable strain within a family and can be the last straw an already tense situation.

In training
Brainstorm ways you can reach and involve all parents, especially the reluctant ones.

To develop trust takes a commitment of time and energy. However, I have realise from my work in both junior and secondary schools that the more informal the contacts I have with the families, the better are my relationships with them. Just going round to a child's house informally for a chat, watching the football team or organising out-of-school activities helped me to relate to the children as human being rather than a remote professional. The 'them' and 'us' barrier exists more than we realise.

If you can find an occasion to talk about the positives with families rather than only when things go wrong, parents will begin to trust you more and feel comfortable about being more involved with their child's education. I remember saying to one child, "What would your mother say if I told her what you just said?" "She wouldn't listen to you," was the reply. I wasn't having that! I visited his house on the way home armed with some good news about his progress. The first time I had to relay it to his mother from the doorstep via his brother. The second time I was invited into the hall, the third time I was asked in for tea. Then I was able to discuss the child's progress fully and establish a relationship with the family that lasted through several members of the family in the school.

If you can find the time to visit the parents who do not come to school, ask their opinions, get them to fill in questionnaires or even tell you about their own school days, they are more likely to feel that they have something to contribute and overcome their reluctance to come to parents' evenings.

Around the School

Schools which impose a set of static rules from above tend to polarise their members into 'them' and 'us'. This can happen to staff and children, teachers and parents or teachers and ancillary staff. Ideally everyone should know what the boundaries are, what will happen if they are crossed and what support there is available. If everyone is consulted and involved in identifying the school rules they will have some commitment and responsibility for making the system work, because they chose it. It also means that everyone knows what is expected of them and what will happen if the rules are broken. A school council, where all the people working in the school are represented, is a good starting point.

Working with Children

6

It is very important to remind ourselves here that we are teachers and not therapists. Our job is to help children to learn, not to sort out their increasingly complicated lives. This is more difficult than it sounds; no doubt we will all find ourselves faced with a needy child and the accompanying desire to 'make things better for them'. But being a counsellor is a skilled job bounded by its professional rules and requirements and it is not the purpose of this book to turn teachers into therapists. If you want to learn and use counselling skills in order that you can work with children in a therapeutic way you need professional counsellor training. (See appendix for useful addresses) *Our job is to create a safe place where children can feel comfortable enough to be able to be who they are, to feel their 'size and shape', and to express their personalities and feel that they are acceptable; we are not qualified to 'sort out' the bits of themselves or their lives that they are unhappy about.*

Up to now we have looked at the processes which lead to the development of maturity and the skills and qualities that a teacher needs to develop in order to facilitate this process in their pupils. If we want the children in our care to develop their individual potential and grow into mature and responsible citizens we have to spend time helping to do this. In order to encourage qualities such as sensitivity and considerateness we need to encounter, and work with the expression of, feelings, values and standards.

For a long time educationalists have looked at factors outside for the causes of any kind of failure within school itself. Some schools respond more effectively to their pupils' need for social development than others and further, some schools have been found even to have a detrimental effect on their pupils! There are areas of pressure which 'affect the quality of experience at school'; factors such as the quality of relationships, the opportunities for pupils to take initiatives and express autonomy have been identified as potential problem areas in schools. Teachers can help counteract negative effects of school through the careful analysis of the kind of environment that has been created and by learning, and using, interpersonal skills.

In training
In pairs, identify the qualities and skills you wish to encourage in your pupils. Share these with the whole group with the intention of refining them to the ones you all agree on.

Group work

Many of the exercises earlier in this book can be used with the children. You can teach them to be assertive, to listen to each other, to manage conflict and to give each other feedback. Group work is one way of teaching these skills. To most teachers, group work means teaching pupils in batches, rather than all at the same time. However, the kind of group work I am describing developed out of the encounter group tradition, in which people would form a group to explore the ways they are thinking and feeling. An encounter group provides certain conditions which facilitate this process of self-expression. Unlike the usual social kind of conversation, there is an absence of 'props' or diversions which normally help us to avoid this kind of interaction. For example, people sit in a circle and only one person talks at a time. There are certain ground rules, mostly negotiated by the group itself about confidentiality, attendance and personal responsibility. The group facilitator keeps the group in touch with what is happening, the process, rather than the content of any communications. In other words, the focus is on how things are expressed not just what is said.

Group work is different from encounter groups because, rather than leave the group members to explore personal issues as they feel moved, exercises, games, role play and discussion are suggested by the facilitator. On a regular basis it needs commitment in terms of staffing and training. However the resources invested would be saved by the reduced need for more specialist support for children whose problems could have been nipped in the bud by the early development of a feeling of belonging and commitment to their peers and community. Group work can be exciting and frightening, it can be like an emotional roller coaster; anything can happen, and it frequently does. So you need to be sure of yourself and your motives and not afraid of getting your 'hands dirty'. If you are creative, can take risks, enjoy being close to people and can handle the ups and downs of relating, it is a unique experience and a very flexible tool.

In these groups, people are able to express some of the hidden parts of themselves in the form of feedback to other people or by self-disclosure. Through this self-expression, they are able to relate to others better and feel more relaxed about themselves. This process can be demonstrated by a Johari Window, a diagram showing the process that takes place in a group. (see over)

The Johari Window

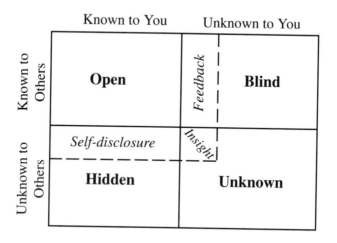

- **Open** area is your open, conscious public behaviour known to you and others.
- **Blind** area is where others can see things about you that you cannot see yourself.
- **Hidden** area represents things we know about ourselves which we do not reveal to others.
- **Unknown** area includes feelings, thoughts and motives within you that are known to niether yourself nor others.

The open area is expanded by talking honestly about ourselves (*self-disclosure*) and listening to *feeback from others.*

Regular meetings?

Group work can take place as part of a tutor group where the young people meet on a regular basis. If you have a regular slot for group work children will get used to it, look forward to it and start to bring their own problems and ideas. If you don't feel it is appropriate to spend regular time working with children in group work you can still use the format for particular occasions like discussing issues and building a 'team spirit'.

Regular group work sessions can be used as a forum for discussion, a basis for establishing ground rules and boundaries and as a way of ensuring that everyone has a say and an opportunity to express their hopes and concerns about what is happening in class or the whole of school. Issues such as bullying and racism can be discussed and, because the children come up with their own solutions, group work is an important way of empowering young people and encouraging them to take responsibility for themselves and what happens in school.

Making groups safe

Before embarking on group work it is important to establish a safe climate by ensuring that everyone knows about, and uses, the core conditions. This can be done by suggesting that, as there is no right and wrong way of doing things, all contributions will be treated with respect. Some ways of doing things may be more appropriate or effective in certain situations; it is up to the group members to convince each other if they feel strongly about a particular way of doing things. It is also important to stress the difference between constructive criticism and put-downs, and ensure that no-one uses group work as an opportunity to scape-goat or show up another member. When children talk about themselves, you need to establish rules about confidentiality. Teachers need to join in the exercises and games too; it is important that if you expect children to take risks, that you are prepared to take them yourself! (See suggested reading in the last section of this book.)

Children may bring up problems of a personal nature, which you, not being a psychotherapist, will probably be unable to deal with. In cases like these you need to develop a strategy for referring the student on to someone who can help, and a way of doing it that is comfortable for both you and the child.

Establishing boundaries and ground rules in group work

Before embarking on a new project, at the beginning of the school year, or when the children seem responsive during a lesson you can use group work to establish or redefine the dos and don'ts of the particular situation. For example, a teacher I know realised that there was a group of children in a particular class who were regularly cracking so many jokes that it was becoming difficult to concentrate on the job in hand. He decided to stop everything and establish some boundaries and ground rules. He told them why he was doing this and they negotiated the following:

- only one person should talk at a time
- in each session they had to get through a certain amount of work
- each child should put some effort into making a contribution during the session
- at the end of the lesson, if they liked and had finished the work in hand, they could have a brief joke-telling session.

However, one child pointed out that the boundaries required the children to change but not the teacher. So the teacher asked them how they would like him to change. They suggested that he should smile more and not waffle!

If children come up with conflicting wishes when establishing boundaries and ground rules, try to give them the support to negotiate a solution that everyone feels comfortable with.

Hopes & concerns raised in group work

It is often useful to address hopes and concerns at the same time as boundaries and ground rules. Ask the children to identify what they want to get out of a session, subject or activity. Also encourage them to identify any worries or preoccupations that prevent them from giving all their attention to the matter in hand. Let the children know that you will refer to it when planning your future sessions and at the end of the project to check whether all the issues have been dealt with. It is useful to make a list, mount it on the wall and allow children to add to the list if the need arises, or the children can write these things anonymously if they prefer.

Group work and personal growth

Group work can be used to develop a young person's identity; they begin to build up a picture of themselves, their personality and the effect they have on others. Sensitively facilitated groups will encourage a sense of personal power and self-esteem. By building up a picture of themselves in a non-judgmental atmosphere, children begin to realise their strengths, become aware of the effect they have on others and realise that they can consciously choose particular behaviour to achieve specific results.

See over for exercises.....

Exercises

1. Filling in questionnaires about their personalities, likes/ dislikes, emotions and responses in specific situations can be both fun and a learning experience. Not only do children learn things about themselves, but also, by comparing themselves to others, they begin to realise that everyone is unique and that differences are just that, different, and not that one is better than another. If the differences between children are respected and accepted they learn tolerance.

2. At the beginning of a group session the pupils may arrive with things on their mind that may affect their involvement in the group. A useful exercise to help them 'put these things away' for a while is to get them to write them on a piece of paper and either throw them into a bin if they want to be rid of them or put somewhere for safe keeping till the end of the session when they can be collected. For example, they may have arrived feeling upset because of something that happened in the last lesson, and rather than carry that upset into the group the feelings can be written on paper and torn up and thrown away to symbolically rid the child of them. Also if the child arrives feeling worried because a member of their family is ill they might not want to have those feelings around during group work but neither do they want to discard them altogether; they can then write their concerns on paper that is kept safe somewhere else for the duration of the group and then picked up again at the end.

3. Categories. One child thinks of another member of the group, but doesn't say who. The rest of the group has to guess who they are thinking of by asking questions like, "If they were a car/animal/flower/rock group what kind would they be?"

4. First impressions. Each child makes a statement about the others. For example, "When I first met Jane I thought she was shy, now I know her better I realise she is just quiet."

5. What if? Members of the group to imagine what each of the others would do in specific situations; if they won the pools, met a destitute person, were invited to a posh party, etc.

6. The token game - In this exercise, the group chooses 10 categories such as 'The person I would tell a secret to', 'The person best at sport', 'The funniest person in the group.' The categories are written on separate pieces of paper and given to the person they think it best fits. Some will get several of the same category, others may get none - points for discussion. Sometimes the children choose categories that could be upsetting for the recipient such as 'The person who is mean.' To prevent this you may feel the need to stipulate that categories should only be nice ones depending on how confident you are about handling any consequent upset and turning it into a positive rather than a negative experience for the recipient and the rest of the group. Discussions like these give children a sense of perspective.

7. Ask the children to remember any thoughts and feelings they have experienced but not expressed to the group. What stopped them?
Divide the group into two halves forming two rows facing each other. Row A walk up to Row B and saying something to the person opposite about the way they have experienced them in the group. The recipient of the feedback should say nothing. Reverse the process. Share with the whole group what it was like not to be able to reply to the feedback and to give the feedback knowing there would be no reply.

Resolving Issues

Group work can also be used to explore particular problems and provoke discussion as to alternative strategies of behaviour. Again a word of warning you may get more than you bargained for if you have a free-for-all. Children may feel safe enough to tell you some things that as their teacher you may not feel comfortable knowing, if they've committed crimes or taken drugs for example. You will need to have thought out your own solutions to these problems beforehand and discussed it with them in the boundaries and ground rules session under the heading of 'Confidentiality', i.e. what you can and can't keep confidential. Find out, as a matter of urgency, your school's policy on what you should do if a child reveals abuse to you.

Exercises

1. 'What would you do if....?' games. Particular situations are written on cards. Each player turns over a question and has to answer it. Then others can make alternative suggestions and discuss the implications of particular responses.

2. Role play of situations that the children have found themselves in, e.g. head teacher's study, in trouble with the police, talking to a friend whose parent is very ill, etc. It is useful to allow the children to choose the characters, and describe their personalities and the sequence of events before acting out a particular scene.

3. Discussion of issues such as bringing up children, bullying, death, racism, marriage, from personal experience with an acknowledgement of feelings.

4. 'What do I need when.....I'm in the house alone, I'm in pain, I've got exams?' situations on cards which must be answered by each member of the group.

> 5. Worst/best case scenario. Looking at the consequences of decisions and actions. "If you get £100 for your birthday, what's the best and the worst thing you could do with it?"

Communication skills for children
Listening skills
To develop reflective listening in the group, you can use some of the exercises earlier in this book.

> **Exercises**
> 1. Working in pairs ask the children to tell their partner what they did, for example, on their holiday, their hobbies, about their pets, etc. Then each child reports as much as they can remember of their partner's words to the group. It is useful to encourage the children to notice and report back on the feelings as well as the words and to check their accuracy with their partner.
>
> 2. When two children are having a dispute, ask them to pretend to be the other person and tell the group what the other person is thinking and feeling using 'I' and 'me' to add to the reality.

Teaching assertiveness to children
If you are assertive with children they will learn to be more assertive for themselves. If you decide to teach assertiveness skills to your pupils, it will help them to deal more constructively with the problems they come up against in their relationships. It will also increase their self-esteem by helping them to feel positive about themselves and their ability to express their feelings and opinions. However, both at school and at home, it is non-assertiveness that is considered 'good' behaviour. *Discussions about when assertive behaviour is*

appropriate and would produce a positive response, would need to be an important part of their training.

If *you* feel offended by a child being assertive, ask yourself "Why?" It could be that you are following an outdated rule true when you were a child but not necessarily appropriate now, for example, the 'rule' that adults should never give in to children or that 'Little children should be seen and not heard.' If you can take a child's wishes seriously, then they can learn to take themselves seriously.

Communicating in times of conflict

A lot of the trouble that arises between children and authority figures escalates from small conflicts in which the children are unable to communicate. Consequentially, they become angry, frustrated and very often abusive. A small incident then becomes a major one. For such situations I have used role-play which gives the young people an opportunity to tell their side of the story and to practise handling the situations they identified as flash points. Situations in which, for example, they are confronted by a teacher about arriving late or about their lack of school uniform. The beauty of this way of working is that during the role play of the original incident, the young people sometimes offer the alternative strategies and this is far more effective than any number of ideas from an adult. They also get a chance to role-play the part of the teacher and this gives them some insight into the other person's point of view.

Exercise

To set up this kind of role play, ask one child to tell a story about themselves, then s/he chooses the people to play the different characters. They go through the story once, then do it a second time and allow the rest of the group to offer alternative behaviours that could have been more effective, or less provocative of conflict.

More exercises

1. If a child is feeling angry you can ask some of the others to make a close circle around her and ask her to try to push her way out.

2. Get everyone to relax and close their eyes and imagine being a member of the opposite sex. What did they do? Where did they go? How did it feel, different or the same?

3. The empty chair. Imagine that a person who gives you trouble is sitting in the chair. Tell them what you think of them, the things that you are never able to say face to face. Then sit in the chair and respond to your own words as if you were the other person. Continue until you can negotiate a truce or some resolution for yourself.

4. Write a letter to someone who is troubling you, no holds barred. Then if appropriate make the letter more reasonable and even post it!

5. Life stories. Tell your life story, draw your life story. Make a map of your life story as though it was a road with the events marked on it.

6. Paint your feelings. Ask the children to close their eyes and relax for a while. Then paint whatever comes to them, quickly, without too much thinking about it. They can discuss, in pairs what the picture looks like for them, and their partner can practise their reflective listening skills.

About the exercises

I have heard the criticism that some of these exercises are 'wet and middle class' or 'Californian' and it is true there are some strange exercises in use. But it is useful to remember that every exercise will fit somewhere; will fit in some place, at some time, in some group. It is important that teachers match the exercise to the group they have in mind - and this requires sensitivity and experience.

Practise doing the exercises first with some adults so that you are aware of some of the risks involved. It is important too, to deal with your own problems before you can work effectively with other people exploring theirs. It is a good idea for you to be a member of a group too to develop yourself and to provide knowledge and insight via personal experience. You might consider doing an introduction to counselling course, these usually last for about 10 sessions, with 3hrs per session.

****

A reminder. Group work is a learning tool. It should not be seen as a psychotherapeutic device, at least not in the hands of teachers. Your aim should always be to develop confidence, respect for others and a sense of belonging to a community.

Teacher Appraisal 7

When teacher appraisal was first discussed I tried to ignore it, hoping it would go away. I assumed that it could only mean more red tape, or worst still, be like some of my worst memories of teaching practice, with someone occasionally sweeping into my classroom with no idea of what I was trying to achieve, jumping to conclusions and giving me tips from their ivory tower. Except that appraisal had a worse feel to it because it felt as though keeping my job depended on it going well.

I was not against the notion of some kind of support for teachers and I could see the sense of the idea that there should be a way of identifying teachers who are unsuited to the job. But I was suspicious of anything that could be linked to assessments and merit awards. I had no faith that it could mean recognition for good work, I worried that it could be used as a way of getting rid of people who challenge the institution, or those who aren't coping because they are left without support.

I have often envied social workers their regular supervision sessions. The opportunity to talk things over with someone who is in a position to offer support and advice. But it did not occur to me that teacher appraisal could offer something like that to teachers.

Around that time my attention was caught by an advert for teacher appraisal trainers. It suggested that a counselling background would be useful. This was interesting! An appraisal programme genuinely based on the counselling principles of respect, genuineness and empathy could be useful after all.

I did some research and discovered that Manchester Education Authority wanted their Teacher Appraisal Programme to be based on sound management techniques. Rather than rely on the government's basic recommendations, they had set up a pilot scheme to investigate the matter fully. It was run in conjunction with the Counselling Careers and Development Unit, based at Leeds University that had been providing training in teacher appraisal for some time. They had developed an appraisal process based on the ideas of Carl Rogers, taking into account the recommendations of the National Steering Group, and which had the blessing of all the teaching unions. It seemed genuine, but even so I was still suspicious.

I answered the advert and when I went for the interview I was determined to voice my reservations. To my surprise the panel seemed to welcome them. As I found out more about the programme, I realised that they really were committed to giving a service that would empower and inform teachers of their rights and responsibilities so that they could get the best from the appraisal process. Issues of equality of opportunity are addressed. Teachers are made aware of the fact that line management now has an acknowledged responsibility to recognise good work and identify and cater for staff-training needs.

The programme itself takes the teachers through each stage of the appraisal process. Both the appraisers and appraisees are trained together to facilitate the trust and respect so necessary for its effectiveness. By asking the teachers to identify their concerns, hopes and objectives both about the appraisal process and the course itself, the reservations and wishes of the teachers are respected. Experiential exercises and videos, rather than 'chalk and talk' are used to identify and practise the various skills required for each stage of the appraisal process and to look at any issues that arise either for the teachers or the school.

After having taken part in the training in several schools, judging from the feedback, the experience seemed useful and enjoyable for teachers. The opportunity for staff teams to get together in a climate of the core conditions to talk about issues that concerned them seemed, in most schools, a useful exercise in its own right. As far as teacher appraisal was concerned, teachers realised that it does not have to be something done to them, but something they can participate in.

The best bit of feedback, for me, was from a teacher who had been very nervous - this was her first day back at work after being off for four years with her young children. By they end of the course she was relaxed and looking forward to her appraisal. Another told us that she had expected to learn something about the process and her own teaching skills, but what she hadn't expected was to find out more about herself as a person.

If you think about it, teacher appraisal has been going on anyway, but unofficially, when, for example, heads and inspectors have written references and discussed teachers with each other. Now this process is in the open. A teacher should be aware of anything that is written about them, and have the opportunity to make their own comments.

By 1st September 1995, all teachers are to have started their appraisal process. Most teacher appraisal is coming to the end of its first two-year cycle. Education authorities have responded to this process in different ways, although as far as I know, all of them have consulted the unions. Some authorities have implemented programmes based on the minimum government requirements and for example, they train only the appraisers, allocate no time for self-assessment or an initial meeting between the appraiser and the appraisee. Others have implemented the whole package and incorporated it into their staff management and development programme.

Whichever kind of appraisal your local authority offers, it helps if you are aware of your rights and the aims and objectives of the appraisal process. However well intentioned a training programme is, it cannot automatically produce skilled and non-judgmental listeners, nor can it ensure that the spirit of the process is necessarily adhered to. If you know what your rights are you can be active in asking for them and recognising when the process is being implemented in an unfair or manipulative way.

Teachers' rights
• to record your own comments on your appraisal statement,
• to indicate that you are content with the statement,
• to have a copy of the statement,
• to training for identified needs,
• to complain within four weeks of the end of the process,
• to a review of your appraisal process by an independent, review officer,
• to confidentiality.

The components of the appraisal process
The process may also include:
• an initial meeting between the appraiser and appraisee,
• self-appraisal and the collection of data from sources, agreed with the appraisee, other than classroom observation,
• classroom observation,
• an appraisal interview in which targets for action are established,
• the preparation of an appraisal statement,
• follow-up including a review meeting between the appraiser and appraisee.

The appraisal statement should be written separately from the agreed targets. The chair of the governing body and LEA training sections can be shown your targets only, on request. A local education authority representative designated by the chief education officer and the head teacher are entitled to a copy of the whole document, i.e. statement plus targets.

The appraisal should be set in the context of the objectives of the school, which will be expressed in the school development plan. Professional development targets should meet the needs of the school as well as the individual appraisees. Appraisal must be seen to operate fairly and equitably for all school teachers and should be undertaken on the basis of an established job description.

A resume of the education regulations for the aims of School Teacher Appraisal:
- to recognise achievements and help teachers to identify ways of improving their skills and performance,
- to assist teachers in their professional development and career planning, where possible, through appropriate in service training,
- to assist teachers to realise their potential and carry out their duties more effectively,
- to identify where a change of duties would help professional development and improve career prospects,
- to help teachers who have difficulties with their performance through training, counselling and appropriate guidance,
- to inform those who have to write references,
- to improve the management of schools.

Epilogue

I believe that childhood experiences can influence us for the rest of our lives. It is a battle to achieve a feeling of self-worth when our experiences lead us to believe that we are worthless; a battle that many people lose. A warm and caring childhood is the surest way of producing a healthy and balanced adult. A person who feels that they have some value is more likely to be able to weather the ups and downs that life dishes out, more able to co-operate with others in a genuine way and more prepared for living a principled life. A child who feels unwelcome, unimportant, judged and found wanting, will take these messages inside and live accordingly. If guilt, anxiety and fear are used to control children, they will grow into worried, fearful or abusive adults. It seems to me there is no other way of looking at it.

Yet, it is difficult to be accepting of children's fears if we are fearful ourselves, or help them find out who they are, if we don't know ourselves. It is difficult, too, to be tolerant and warm when we don't feel that we have been accepted and valued. One generation has collectively to break the vicious circle and give consciously, willingly and joyfully what they didn't receive when they were children. Let it be ours.

Useful Addresses & Information

Further reading

Axline, V. (1964) *Dibbs: In Search of Self*, Pelican Books. GB.

Brandes, D. & Phillips, H. (1985) *Gamesters' Handbook,* Hutchinson.

Brandes, D. & Phillips, H. (1982) *Gamesters' Handbook 2,* Hutchinson.

Dillon, J.T. (1971) *Personal Teaching*, Charles Merrill Pub Co. Ohio.

Gazda, G. (1973) *Human Relationship Development*, Allyn & Bacon Inc. Boston.

Houston, G. (1984) *The Red Book of Groups,* The Rochester Foundation, 8 Rochester Place, London.

McGuiness, J. & Craggs, D. (1986) *Management of Disruptive Pupil Behaviour in Schools*, John Wiley & Sons Ltd. Canada.

Morrison, A. & McIntyre, D. (1984) *Teachers & Teaching*, Routledge & Kegan Paul. London.

Nash, R. (1976) *Teacher Expectation & Pupil Learning*, Routlegde & Kegan Paul. London.

Riddel, S. & Brown, S. (1991) *School Effectiveness Research*, H.M.S.O. Edinburgh.

Rogers, C.R. (1951) *Client-Centred Therapy*, Constable & Co Ltd. London.

Rogers, C.R. (1983) *Freedom to Learn for the 80s*, Charles E. Merrill. Columbus, Ohio.
Rogers, C.R. (1980) *A Way of Being*, Houghton Mifflin. Boston.
Sanders, P. (1994) *First Steps in Counselling*, P.C.C.S. Manchester.
Thorne, B. (1992) *Carl Rogers*, Sage Publications Ltd. London.
Winnicot, D.W. (1971) *Playing & Reality*, Tavistock. London.

Suppliers of relevant resources

The Chalkface Project,
P.O.Box 907,
Milton Keynes,
MK13 8YU

Rapport Learning Ltd.
1st Floor,
6 Langley Street
London
WC2H 9JA

Both these addresses can supply teaching materials for assertiveness training, etc. to use with children.

The Family Directory ISBN 0-7521-0117-X (£1.00) contains relevant information and addresses. Available from book shops or from:
Customer Services, Health Education Authority, Hamilton House, Mabledon Place, London WC1H 9TX Tel 071 413 1946

Useful addresses and phone numbers

British Association for Counselling
Counselling in Education Division
1 Regent Place
Rugby
Warks
CV21 2PJ
Tel 0788 550899

Chris Doyle
Deputy Head
The Alfred Barrow School
Duke Street
Barrow-in-Furness
Cumbria
LA14 2LB
Tel 0229 827355

Janette Newton
Teamleader
Counselling Service
Westox House
1 Trinity Road
Dudley
W. Mids
DY1 1JB
Tel 0384 452361

Parent Network
44-46 Caversham Road
London
NW5 2DS
Tel 071 485 8535
Fax 071 267 4426
Offers training courses for parents that would be equally useful for
teachers.

PCCS
Paragon House
Seymour Grove
Old Trafford
Manchester
M16 0BE
Tel/Fax 061 877 9877
Offers advice and consultancy regarding setting up in-service training, and for those within reach of Manchester, counselling training courses at all levels.

Childline
2nd Floor
Royal Mail Building
Studd Street
London
N1 0QW
Tel 071 239 1000
Fax 071 239 1001
Helpline: 0800 1111

Parentline
Westbury House
57 Hart Road
Thundersley
Essex
SS7 3PP
Helpline: 0268 757077   9am-6pm Mon-Fri   10am-2pm Sat
afterhours numbers supplied on answerphone.
There are local branches of Parentline, the contact numbers of which will be available from the helpline number above.
Provides support for parents under stress.